Organisation and business change draws from the language and practices coming from navigation. In doing so it borrows from a rich history and creative discipline that enables people to move across our incredible planet home.

This book explores the principles, practices and capability that need to inform our understanding of how to navigate in today's changing world. The World Economic Forum and others are calling for leaders to be able to 'navigate in uncharted waters'. Leaders can only do this successfully, if first of all they have a deep understanding of what it is to navigate.

As a former captain of passenger ferries who has worked in business for the last thirty years it is my hope that I can illuminate this critical area for leaders. I want to challenge some of the less helpful patterns that so many of us see currently and also give a practical hope that things can be different. For those who are getting it right, I want to encourage them to keep going and keep learning.

Chris Lever

Navigating Change. A Leader's Guide

Copyright 2018 Chris Lever
All rights reserved
Printed in the UK
Distributed by Teleios Consulting Ltd
Designed by Will Morse

Permission can be requested from Chris by mailing
chrislever@teleiosconsulting.com

This book is dedicated to firstly my Dad, Royal Marine, Coxswain and Engineer. Together we loved wild places, big skies and restless seas. And to Bob Hale, Master Shipwright, captain, friend and mentor who taught me how to navigate.

Contents

Foreword:
A salutary lesson – David Oliver

As I write this foreword, the UK's BBC News is firing another round of missiles at the ineptitude of rail companies. With apparently stunning incompetence they launched a new timetable overnight across the whole country. No-one really understood why it was being done, none of the millions of paying customers had clarity around what trains would be where; and over many days, thousands of scheduled trains have simply been cancelled. One of the reasons for this situation is a dramatic shortage of train drivers to run the newly timetabled additional services.

The country is in uproar. The Secretary of State for transport is coming under pressure to resign and the sense of national embarrassment, incredulity and rage over this incompetence is growing apace. Surely someone somewhere had worked out how many trains there were and how many drivers were needed? This is primary school maths! Along with the real outrage there is a call for accountability from those responsible for this avoidable debacle.

The unfolding mess beggars belief!

What this sorry story reflects is a wider reality. From all the data available, as best we know, a very high percentage (between 60 and 80%, depending on which study is being looked at) of change programmes fail to deliver fully on their aspirational goals. In other words, this railway mishap is sadly the norm not the exception. Currently 50% of Digital Transformation programmes fail completely. The feelings caused by this very public shambles are understandable and yet the same outrage and uproar currently being vented on the hapless rail officials, is rarely meted out to leaders who fail to lead and manage change effectively in their organisations. Very few of those leaders and their teams are ever held to account, and this sorry cycle repeats itself unnecessarily, over and over again, leaving a trail of formerly motivated, committed, generous hearted staff members in burn out or disappointment.

That's why this book is a must read

I have been a businessman and consultant for four decades. I have had the privilege of working with some of the world's largest and best corporations. I have also had the huge privilege of working with the public sector, many hundreds of SMEs, charities and not-for-profits. My observation aligns with the data. Over 40 years of observation very few of the many hundreds of change initiatives I have witnessed have delivered what their originators intended. This success rate of change is very low and, in the failure, lurk the many stories of missed opportunities and real hardship. And the truth is that so much of this could have been avoided because the knowledge and data so necessary for good navigation was there before the start of the change, if only the leaders had eyes to look and the wit to understand. Of course the switched on leaders have already figured this out which is why they outperform the rest.

This book addresses this reality unlike any other book on change I've read. It has what I would call a 'prophetic illumination'. It shines an uncomfortably bright light onto the personal and corporate sources of change failure, and challenges us to respond. The author Chris Lever then gives us a well-tested time-honoured set of three principles and their associated tool's, which allow leaders to calibrate, cross reference and drive out error. These approaches are easy to understand and easy to remember. The text is uncompromising in some ways but has hope written right through it. The current state doesn't need to be like it is.

Drawing from his time as a passenger ferry captain and decades of experience with some of the biggest change programmes around, Chris draws from the 3 principles of skilled navigation enabling every reader to….

1 figure out where they are on a range of different measures, driving out as much error as they can…

2 be able to articulate vision with clarity, confidence and realism, breathing life into often weary bones…..

3 and then be able to make sense of the complexity of the way ahead, understanding the nature of the systemic risks and opportunities without getting stuck in them.

This translates into being able to prioritise choices. This also requires leaders to be well connected to all stakeholders, be able to read the way ahead and respond with agility so that all actions and choices are informed, intentional and intelligent.

A renewed confidence to handle any change

Chris has written from decades of authentic experience in change projects and programmes. His integrity, honesty and vulnerability will challenge you and then provide hope. The book will also provoke you and then provide you with practical approaches and achievable outcomes. You will finish up feeling a new or renewed sense of confidence that in turn will do others good and will do organisations and businesses good.

And if it impacts you as it has me, you might find yourself giving away more copies of this book than any other book you have read.

David Oliver
Businessman, Author, Keynote Speaker
Whitchurch Hampshire UK

Introduction

With unparalleled levels of change taking place in all sectors across the world there is a need for our leaders to be able to skilfully navigate in complex and ever shifting global conditions. In an increasing number of cases they are required to find their way in what seems like 'unfamiliar waters'.

Navigation is an activity close to my heart. As a former passenger ferry captain, it has a particular resonance and interest for me. I have, along with most seafarers, a specific understanding of what the term 'to navigate' means and entails.

When I changed career direction and joined one of the leading US computer corporations some time ago, I was pleased to discover the language of navigation was being used to describe business activities. What I also noticed was that the precision and demands that I associate with this discipline were often poorly understood. I continue to work with organisations across the world and this is still my observation. It is this that I feel is having a serious impact on the ability to deliver successful change.

The World Economic Forum (WEF) states that success in finding a way through the 'unknown waters' of Digital Transformation is dependent on the ability of leaders to navigate with skill and some courage. The WEF, along with others, is suggesting that we may need to rethink what is required of leaders at this time. I would suggest that this is true for *all* change, as well as that associated with the 'Fourth Industrial Revolution', as some are describing it (Schwab, 2015).

I would also like to assert from the outset that being able to navigate without charts, first of all is wholly dependent on mastery of a broad range of navigational principles and practices. Given a choice I would always want to work from accurate and up to date maps, but where these are either absent or of poor quality I will rely on all of my other skills to find good passage. This is what this book explores.

I have worked with very talented and inspirational men and women over the years and I have come to respect them immensely. They create and preside in 'Change-Able' organisations that have learnt how to succeed from one situation to the next. These organisations look and feel so different from the norm. The leaders skilfully and intuitively find good passage through the competing demands and high-cost sandbanks that lurk just below the surface of their markets and areas of work.

They are informed. They are intentional. They also work with a sparkling intelligence.

However these enterprises only represent a relatively small percentage of organisations across the world. A significant proportion of leaders and leadership teams just don't seem to have an adequate working knowledge of the principles of navigation with the depth and breadth required by the situation, or indeed their ambition. Perhaps they have never been introduced to the discipline and this is resulting in some strange behaviour and decisions.

Some leaders, too, seem to have either forgotten what they have learnt, or choose not to apply this knowledge.

This is also contributing to the considerable failure rates of programmes designed to leverage uplifts in performance. This is having an impact on 'UK plc' and our ability to engage in the challenges of today.

The good news however is that this aspect of change can be fixed if there is the desire, and if people are prepared to develop the knowledge, skills and attitudes so vital for success.

For this reason I felt it was the right time to describe core navigational practices and key activities and show how they relate to business and organisational life. It is my hope that leaders of change can increase the depth of their capability as well as extend the breadth. And the encouragement is that this is achievable if there is the *will* to do so.

First of all... taking a broader look

When I reflect on the journey from deckhand to skipper, along with the formal qualifications and continual assessment, I remember that I was encouraged to take a broad interest in things that might, at first glance, seem a little way from navigational skills.

For example, I learnt how to 'feel' and pay attention to subtle shifts in wind speed/direction, and temperature.

Along with a growing understanding of weather patterns this meant I was prepared early, for shifts in conditions. My mentor took me around shipyards to watch how the vessel I was later to command was designed and built. This gave insights into capability and handling. I was continually shown how to read the 'here and now' and extrapolate this across different time lines. Through this I learnt to make use of scenario thinking and planning. I became fascinated with observing bird behaviour and migration patterns. This proved useful to my understanding of early changes in weather and sea conditions. I was also coached in observing human behaviour in order to work effectively with all sorts and styles. Along with everything else I developed a real love of history. I spent many hours chatting over tea and coffee listening to the stories of dockworkers and fishermen and women recounting tales from living memory. This then developed into a lifelong interest in the movement by land and sea of our early ancestors. I learnt that 'navigating in uncharted waters' is not quite the new, challenge for leaders that some might have us believe, but instead is as old as our human story itself. This is strangely comforting.

> // **Change and transition can be looked at through a variety of lenses each providing a richness of view and understanding.**

All of this curiosity was outworked in a company and business that believed in development and where 'high support and high challenge' was the daily norm.

Learning was and still is a personal delight. And all of these elements contributed to my ability to navigate the choices I had to make with my crew on a minute-by-minute basis. In fact I would say drawing on this width of experience and knowledge was critical to the quality and speed of decisions required of me every day.

It is my observation, therefore, that leading change and transition also calls for a breadth of interest and understanding from a range of disciplines. In fact I would argue that it is essential and critical for overall success. Change can be looked at through a variety of lenses each providing a richness of view and understanding. These include:

- Understanding shifts in human history that followed either the introduction of a new technology, or how people and communities responded to 'events'.

- Seeing organisations as a system with interconnections, multiple pathways and diverse relationships.

- Insights from neuroscience and physiology into how individuals and systems function and conform to patterns, and how behaviour can be 'rewired'. Plasticity is good news but offers a massive challenge, as repitition takes time to embed new behaviours and attitudes.

- Mathematics and particularly the study of fractals can help our exploration of repeating cultural patterns and why they are just so hard to shift.

- Scenario thinking and working helps us to work predictively, with foresight.

- Swarm theory provides insights into how organisations seem to take on an intelligence (or lack of it) and persona of their own.

- Digital transformation, artificial intelligence and robotics are all offering game changing advancements along with many dilemmas.

- Emotional intelligence (EI) provides a language and ways to help us understand and positively connect with other people.

- Creativity provides the energy and possibilities of change.

- Data is becoming the new unit of currency and again offers great potential advancements and some very tough decisions.

And the list could go on...

The point is that there is a richness offered by studying a range of disciplines associated with change, which in turn will open up a whole world of research, insights and practical applications. Just like at sea, the quality of decisions and speed of decision taking can be enhanced if a leader draws on relevant and interconnected sources of information. This is about getting the right things done well the first time. Being curious is so important, as it is often in the combination of different disciplines that breakthroughs also happen. Of course for the leader or practitioner the aim is to know *enough* to be informed, to be able to make the right decisions... and understand where the limits of our own understanding run out. Which is why we need other people to add knowledge and experience, to argue, to collaborate, to dialogue with and to jointly care about the journey ahead as well as the outcome.

> **The point is that there is a richness offered by studying a range of disciplines associated with change which will open up a whole new world.**

Why is this important?

From a practical point of view, the above offers a way of making sense of the world which in turn creates traction and acceptance, which in turn creates momentum avoiding delays; it also helps our understanding of how the whole needs to work together and how we must never to lose sight of the fact that it is people who are at the centre of all effort.

This is all about increasing successful outcomes and reducing the failure rate of change programmes – and the failure rate is very high. The majority of programmes never fully see the anticipated uplifts talked about at the start. Half of Digital Transformation initiatives fail completely and just under half of mergers and acquisitions actually destroy shareholder value. The cost of this on finances, time and people is unacceptably high. At a time when we need to be very competitive in our work, opportunity is being lost.

This book will therefore draw on a variety of disciplines.

The focus however is very much about how leaders navigate, or find their way, in ever changing conditions, taking their businesses and organisations with them on what is effectively an adventure and journey of discovery.

Before exploring in some depth the three underpinning and core navigational principles and how they apply to business, I want to continue taking a wider view of the territory of change. The first section therefore is a little montage representing various facets specific to navigation. I guess it could be described as a 'trip around the bay', as it explores very important parts, that together make up the territory of change and transformation.

It also hints at the development that is required for leaders who have the responsibility to find a way through the many choices and options, that face them everyday.

To navigate

This first section I have described as a montage of insights and perspectives. Understanding the territory of change as well as the development of the leader as navigator can be looked at from multiple viewpoints. Linked together they create an intricate but connected picture.

Navigation is the art and science of finding a way through a territory on land, sea and air. At a deeper level it is also about finding a way through the mixed ambitions of people and their individual drivers, including our own. At its most fundamental it is all about making a continuous stream of choices to help maintain the course towards our intended and hoped for destination.

This first section draws on a personal story, observations, research and trending developments. Understanding the territory of change, as well as the journey of development of the navigator / leader should be viewed from multiple and interconnected standpoints. I am aware that in this first positioning piece I move around subjects with some fluidity! For this reason I offer with this section and throughout the book Waymarks to help navigate the text.

Waymarks to navigate this section

Waymarks are a navigator's device to help steer the vessel. They represent known places in a seascape where distance, rough weather, poor visibility or busy shipping lanes could be obscuring the next stage of the passage. They are also used to provide confidence that we are making progress against an intentional plan.

Change is the new constant

Very occasionally I come across a rare individual who believes that the latest change programme they are going through will be the last for some while. They continue to hope that 'things will eventually return to normal'. This view in organisations is now pretty uncommon as most accept that change is the new normal and also the new constant.

Whilst there is an acceptance of change becoming the usual backdrop of all of our work, the figures reveal we aren't very good at leveraging the opportunity afforded by new ways and new ideas. The majority of change and Digital Transformation programmes fail to deliver the anticipated outcomes with an average of no more than 15% of organisations being truly 'Change-Able' (the term used in Atticus's ChangeAbility Research from which the data I am using comes from. See section notes on page 84).

So organisations that figure out how to make shifts effectively minimising disruption, reducing time taken to establish new patterns and delivering on strategic outcomes will flourish... and indeed are flourishing. These ever changing times will sift out the Change-Able and those who are Change-Inept, or Change-Ineffective (Atticus, n.d.).

The Change-Ineffective enterprises will continue to lurch from initiative to initiative. They will spend vast sums of money retrofitting solutions that are never quite as effective as doing it right first time around and in the meantime will have seriously upset both customers and employees. And then everything will be reorganised in the hope of fixing the issues, and of course it never does...

Along with Digital Transformation approaching like a relentless tsunami, it must be noted that we seem to be in a vortex of wider change, causing disruption to the rhythms and patterns that make up life on our planet home. Some of these shifts offer progress and hope and others are raising serious questions. Climate change is causing disruptive shifts in weather patterns across the world and is already having impact on life and business. Geopolitical changes are throwing up some shifts that would not have been on most people's radars a few years ago. The economic hubs and structures are moving around with some fluidity. Science is offering the tantalising prospect of fusion power and also autonomous machines and robotics… to name just a few.

So for those who like stability, the next decades will be challenging!

We are so obviously living in extraordinary times that are presenting pretty important options and some equally hard choices for us all. The only thing that feels consistent is that the rate of change and its range and depth continues to accelerate exponentially. The question is how are we going to respond?

As leaders we have to figure out how to navigate in this emerging and only partly understood age in which we find ourselves doing business. Organisations like the World Economic Forum are identifying that a key leadership differentiator in the future will be the 'ability to navigate in uncharted waters'. As a qualified navigator I know this is a big ask. It can be done but will demand significant depth of capability and experience… and some wisdom. I think we also need to start rethinking, the training, coaching and the development of this discipline as well as being able to assess the leaders' capability to deliver.

Industrial revolutions:
Lessons from the past, applied now
There are a growing number of voices that are saying that the 'fourth industrial age' the Digital Transformation we are currently living through will bring unprecedented levels of change the like of which we have not experienced before.

My colleague Ross Harling, a senior EU analyst, continually reminds me that Digital Transformation will reach further, be faster, paradoxically take longer and go deeper than much of our experience to date. So, if it has been felt that organisational life has been a bit fluid over the past years as we adapt to and adopt, new ideas and new ways, the emerging reality is…

… that we haven't seen anything yet!

Klaus Schwab, founder of the World Economic Forum, says in an article first published in 2015 in Foreign Affairs:

'We stand on the brink of a technological revolution that will fundamentally alter the way we live, work, and relate to one another. In its scale, scope and complexity, the transformation will be unlike anything humankind has experienced before. We do not yet know how it will unfold, but one thing is clear: the response to it must be integrated and comprehensive, involving all stakeholders of the global polity, from the public and private sectors to academia and civil society.'

As an enthusiastic historian I know that times of change from one era to another and from one technology to another is the stuff of our human story.

From stone to copper to bronze to iron… from Roman centralisation and standardisation to the almost invisible footprint of the Anglo Saxons… our history has always featured times of great transition which have altered the fabric of life. And then of course there is the example of how a seemingly small event like the introduction of the horse stirrup, courtesy of the Vikings, ended up reshaping the very landscape of the British Isles and creating the new and titled landed classes. However that is a story best told by Dr Helen Geake, archaeologist and finds adviser at Cambridge University (Taylor, 2006, pp.152-153).

The first Industrial Revolution used water and steam to usher in mechanisation. Part of this story is beautifully told by Alan Villiers in his book, Set of the Sails (1973). Alan was a businessman, ship owner and captain. He worked at the very time when steam was replacing sail. His story of this extraordinary period of transition tells of the great advances in ship design and sailing practices that produced some of the most efficient sailing ships ever built. This was the old industry's response to the competitive times it found itself trading in. For a period the old technology out-performed the new but then steam engines matured, ship design advanced and finally these new vessels left the likes of the Cutty Sark in their wake. In his writing Villiers tells of the sadness as old ways of life came to an end, and he describes the emerging hope that many saw in the new vessels and trade opportunities.

//// **The old ways reimagined and brought to life with new technologies are finding a critically important place once again.**

What is extraordinary is that what was once a tussle between old and new technologies, has recently found a new symbiotic relational relevance for today's challenges. The modern cruise liner business is both expanding and experiencing increasing criticism as a major contributor of pollution. So the ship designers have returned to the age of sail to look for less environmentally harmful propulsion systems. The solution though is far from old school sails and canvass. The Viking Grace, a state of the art Finnish passenger ship uses a revolutionary rotor sail to work along aside the ships engines in order to reduce the amount of fuel used and reduce too the emissions. This design is now being rolled out across many cruise ships. The reduction in fuel consumption is significant. So this is great for cutting costs and great for the environment too. The old ways reimagined and brought to life with new technologies are finding a critically important place once again.

In the article written by Klaus Schwab (2015) on behalf of the WEF, there are echoes of Alan Villiers' book. Of course there is different content, scales and reach. But here lies our challenge... Alan wrote Set of Sails in 1949 after he, and the world, had begun to make sense of the era they had lived through and reached reflective and considered conclusions. The fourth industrial revolution is happening now so our challenge is to try to figure it out whilst being in the middle of the transition. This may not be an easy thing to do!

What we do glimpse however is that Digital Transformation will have a far-reaching impact on all facets of our lives. One of many questions that some are beginning to ask is how our human decision making processes work and interface with fully automated and artificially intelligent systems that are capable of working independently of us. Changes to the way we do things will indeed be massive and will pose questions that go way beyond technology. It's interesting to listen to someone like the late great Stephen Hawking (2016) as he shares some of his fears for the future arising from robotics and artificial intelligence, and then listen to the tech visionaries and corporate technology companies as they share their dreams.

We are all just beginning to understand that the digital revolution will have a huge impact not only on the way business is done, but how it is led, managed and structured.

It will also impact how organisations relate to others in the same sector, and how business uses disruptive ideas from a wide range of quite unrelated fields that will challenge convention. Currently digital advances are outstripping legislation and political and institutional structures. The tech giants are wielding huge power, whether they like it or not, and accountability and responsibility need to catch up.

The reality however is that we are all in catch-up mode.

Klaus Schwab's glimpse into the future raises many questions and as the author asserts, this gives us some important choices. In response to the article the World Economic Forum (2016) states that leaders have to learn to 'navigate' in these unknown and unfamiliar waters.

This brings me back to the central theme of this book....

Enduring navigational principles

The principles that lie at the heart of good navigation are constant.

The enabling technology may have radically evolved and the application will always change in relation to context. But what's involved at the very core is still the same. This is true at sea, where my career started, and is true also of organisations figuring out how to survive and flourish in today's turbulent trading conditions.

Leaders have to navigate through the real world that shapes what we can do in the present and yet hold a hope for an opportunity defined future. And of course that future starts tomorrow. The skill of the leader is therefore tested in his or her ability to navigate through a complex and sometimes uncharted environment from the current location to the desired future and their intentional destination. This is to be achieved without bumping into things, running aground, sinking or running out of fuel.

> /// There is a major difference between being lost with an unskilled leader and being lost with one who does know what they are doing even if they don't know 'at this particular moment' where they are 'currently'. And I know which I prefer to travel with.

We may not have up to date maps or charts for all of the territories ahead, but we do have a compass (organisational and personal equivalents exist) and a whole host of principles, tools and enabling technologies to help us find our way. It is to be hoped too, that leaders will have been increasingly trained and qualified in the discipline of organisational navigation and in the use of the associated toolkit. The subject of navigation has to start appearing more regularly on leadership developmental curriculum and training programmes.

As already stated, currently few change initiatives fully deliver their real and intended advantage. So despite reorganisations, outsourcing core and vital functions, and culture change initiatives, nothing much seems to change substantially. Outright failure rates are high and the cost of retrofitting patches to cover inadequate initial solutions is unbearably high. As a result we are creating greater populations of severely fatigued employees whose goodwill often takes up the strain of change programmes that have been poorly thought through, and who have in the process become cynics. We would do well to remember though that cynics are often people who have once cared deeply but who have been burnt once too often.

I estimate, based on first hand experience, that up to 70% of this failure is down to leaders who have not piloted their organisation with the experience and capability that was needed in these challenging times. I can only conclude that the principles of navigation are either not understood or are not being applied with anywhere near the skill, courage and wisdom that is required.

So, to restate, the reason I have written this book is to help leaders, and those responsible for introducing and implementing change, to navigate more effectively through the multitude of choices that they will have to make. Both the nature, and the sequencing, of many of these choices, is foreseeable much of the time, if we take a moment to 'read' what is going on around us.

In the following sections, I will use the three foundational principles of navigation and apply them to the three fundamental questions that need resolving in any organisational shift. These are then brought to life through experience and crucible moments that have transformed us and our willingness to learn. You can only appreciate what riding out a storm feels like if you have actually ridden out a storm. You can only know the depth of the challenges of trying to shift embedded patterns of organisational behaviour, if you have done this before.

A personal view

Over my working life so far, I have had the pleasure of having a range of very different jobs. There is however a theme running through a career at sea, in academia, in the corporate world and in array of SMEs (small to medium-sized enterprises). I like to push boundaries, to learn, to explore new territories and to bring others through with me.

Change has been a constant and positive experience for me over the years, even if it has been tough making the shift sometimes. Like anyone who has been around a bit I have the scars from failure. I try to allow these times to be my teacher, although I do confess that there have been occasions when I have been a bit slow on the uptake. I have also achieved some good successes, which have been written about by various authors over the past few decades.

Navigation is about making choices based on the best information available and in accord with regulatory demands, the operating context and of course our fundamental beliefs and values. Skilful navigators have learnt to read and make sense of the 'here and now' and also the 'there and then' of the near future. They understand that their vessel is part of a complex system that is ever changing and which will be impacted by the choices they make as leaders. All of this needs to be taken into account throughout the decision making process.

Trending...

In today's ever changing markets and sectors though, I regularly come across two worrying trends:

1 Few organisations have any kind of change architecture informing decisions, direction and culture. They seem to tumble along not knowing what to do when. Employees and other stakeholders experience this as a lack of coherence. It all feels as though there isn't enough joined up thinking that can be trusted or relied upon.

2 As already mentioned, I hear the language and imagery of navigation used frequently. However I just don't see the depth of understanding behind the words that informs successful change. To restate again, as many as 80% of all change programmes fail to deliver fully on their aspirational goals. Currently 50% of Digital Transformation programmes fail completely. If 50% of voyages failed to get to their destination there would be total uproar, multiple enquiries and years of legal actions (see section notes on page 84 re statistics used).

In a recent (2017) book called 'Ensuring change delivers success', I offer and explore an architecture for change, based on the movement between five identifiable phases. This outlines a flow of choices that the leader will have to make over the life span of a programme.

Charts and maps that help us find a way

Maps have always fascinated me as they bring an added understanding and appreciation of a landscape and show how man-made and natural features relate to each other. In a strange way their iconic simplicity adds to our understanding of the real world. I enjoy them too as they allow me to get to interesting places and meet interesting people.

I still have the map of Zimbabwe and Southern Africa that my family and our friends used to explore the region some years ago. The coffee stains and the crumpled edges remind us all of a great adventure. (In fact the coffee stains are a direct reminder of how we started most days. The map would be unfolded onto the bonnet of the truck. Our mugs of coffee would secure the corners and then we would plan the next stage of the adventure, balancing out places we wanted to visit with security risks and distance to be travelled).

The two families always took planning decisions together and shared in the outcomes, most of which had their fair share of adventure. In business terms this was about sharing risk and reward with all stakeholders.

To this day I enjoy using these tools and my wits to find my way around and most of all I like wild places with big skies. Google Earth has mapped the planet with extraordinary detail but there are still places where the maps are pretty inadequate. In these places skill, judgement and experience kick in to help navigate a way through.

Later in this book I will give the example of how the DIY store B&Q produced an extraordinary map over a decade ago. It was stunning in both its simplicity and depth of insight and helped the business navigate through some challenging times and markets. Maps of this quality really do help leaders to navigate successfully. Interestingly, this map was created by them, in their language, for their 'unfamiliar waters'. They achieved this by looking ahead.

However, the brutal honesty that helped them wrestle with big decisions and the skill therefore to imagine the content on what started as a blank canvas is in short supply in many organisations. So where the territory is not just unfamiliar but uncharted there is an even greater need for leaders to have had a grounding in the intricacies of navigation.

And when the map does not exist

To restate again, it is my assertion that navigating through 'uncharted waters' increases the need for leaders and their teams to first of all be highly skilled in navigational principles. Some would infer that in these times of unprecedented change, the old disciplines are no longer relevant. However just the phrase 'navigating in uncharted waters' maintains the need to navigate... but with the absence of a chart or at least of an accurate one.

There is a major difference between being lost with an unskilled leader and being lost with one who does know what they are doing even if they don't know 'at this particular moment' where they are 'currently'. And I know which I prefer to travel with.

As a statement of the obvious, the landscape exists in reality; what doesn't sometimes exist is the map or chart, which is simply a representation of that reality. So at sea I am continually reading the direction of tidal flows, the patterns of waves that may indicate hazards below the surfaces, changes in wind direction/speed and temperature and the sound the vessel is making. All of this allows me to pilot with care without reference necessarily to a chart. Where they exist, charts do help me understand context, relationships between features, distances, obstructions, dangers and opportunities for

interesting pathways. All of this helps me make decisions both ahead of time and in real time. However I don't stop navigating if I don't have either an accurate map or indeed any map at all.

As I have mentioned, I love places with wide horizons and have spent time in these inspiring environments in both the northern and southern hemispheres. Without maps or GPS it is entirely possible to journey through the landscape if you apply core principles and the ability to read information from different sources.

When exploring I do try to go out with at least a compass, but even without this basic bit of kit, if the sun shines I can figure out where north, south, east and west are situated. At night I have stars that provide a directional fix, and if the sun doesn't shine I can figure out direction by reading which side of a tree lichen is growing or, in sand dunes, which way the sand is piling up as long as I know the prevalent wind direction. And there are many 'tells' that provide information about direction if we know what to look out for.

Rivers run downhill so if you are trying to lose elevation this obvious fact is rather helpful. On moorland hillsides purple heather dramatically gives way to the white Molinia grass, defining dry and boggy areas. When all you can see to the horizon is the bog grass Molinia, but running through it are scrub bushes more or less in a line, the probability is that this is an ancient causeway. This means you may have found a route where your feet won't get so wet and where you are less likely to twist an ankle on grass tussocks!

There is always information out there if you can read it. Multiple strands of information, even if it's a bit limited, can be put together to help the 'off chart' navigator make those important decisions.

One of my colleagues from Cranfield Business School came up with the notion of the compass of 'four intelligences' to help navigate through the confusion of business life. Some authors ask 'How emotionally intelligent is your organisation?' and this indeed is a very important question. John Dickson (personal communication. See section notes) includes other cardinal compass points along with EI. So political intelligence (PI) is critical, along with business intelligence (BI). What provides the north cardinal point is spiritual intelligence (SI). John points out that this is not a religious reference but involves a clear set of values or core beliefs that provides our base line for all decisions. An informal study of senior managers over a five-year period at Cranfield Business School indicates that the least developed of the cardinal points in this population are SI and PI.

The north cardinal point is also about core purpose. I may be travelling in uncharted waters but my direction and course will be set to my intended destination. This is why, particularly in these transformational times, it is critical we all have a clearish and an emerging picture of where we are trying to get to. If this is the case we have a decent chance, if we read all of the available information, of going in the right direction even without a chart.

However if we don't know where we are, as well as not knowing where we are trying to get to ...we really will be lost.

An extended feeling of being lost or being continually adrift creates dangerous times for many reasons, including setting a climate that allows some leadership types who are convinced of their own certainty and rightness to grab power and march everyone towards perilous precipices. The rise in the incidence of sociopathic and psychopathic leaders who offer false certainty is I suggest a response to a situation where not enough leaders are able to navigate with skill, courage, humility and wisdom in challenging times. We too as followers and voters should take responsibility for the speed with which we abandon intelligent scrutiny for false hope. The book Snakes in Suites by Paul Babiak and Robert Hare (2006) is a sobering and sometimes disturbing read.

> **So here is a radical thought: if history repeats itself (it has to do so because no one listens first time around), then could we be smart and learn lessons from the past that just may save some present pain?**

There may be no 'high definition maps' for the technological revolution that Klaus Schwab (2015) describes and this is going to prove challenging for all in leadership. However, like the explorers of old we do have navigational principles to apply, we do have experience if we choose to learn from it and we have technology that not only poses challenges but can provide the tools to work with on the issues.

In addition we have the records of past industrial breakthroughs. I have referenced the Alan Villiers book as one source of information that might just help us at this time. I would recommend it as a comparative study. Industrial museums like the one at Ironbridge, along with sociological records and histories, also provide a rich source of information for us. There are patterns tucked into all of this information that repeat over the millennia, as new technologies are introduced, that could help provide at least some outline charts for us in this present time.

So here is a radical thought: if history repeats itself (it has to do so because no one listens first time around), then could we be smart and learn lessons from the past that just may save some present pain?

The journey and the impact of Digital Transformation

With the rate of change seeming to get faster and more demanding across all sectors and geographies, I am still shocked by the number of leaders who set out on their change programmes with little preparation and inadequate tools, plans and resources. Some say you can't plan for something you have no control over. Others still believe that you can simply transfer from point A to point B without 'fussing about the options and people'. It is no wonder therefore that few change initiatives fully deliver on the benefits outlined at the start.

The above situation is compounded further by a lack of robust understanding of how to leverage Digital Transformation (DT). As mentioned, one of my colleagues, amongst other roles, is a EU business analyst and adviser. He has crunched the numbers using data from the EU, OECD, UK Government figures and 'the big four consultancies' and, to restate, he has found that around 80% of Digital Transformation projects are failing to deliver fully on expected results and 50% are failing completely. Wildly unrealistic expectations set by IT vendors, together with an often naïve response from under-pressure potential customers, is hampering what could be achieved in the on-going digital revolution. For many at the present 'DT' is becoming a toxic term based on their experience to date.

This is such a significant dimension of the change agenda that we will deal with it in a separate publication. In the meantime, Ross Harling has written a paper called 'Will your council be a digital dynamo or a dinosaur?' (2017). Although this has been written for the public sector it has wider application.

Three core principles, but just one personal question for many

There are three very important foundational principles that will determine whether a change of any size (transformational, transitional or developmental) is likely to succeed. However for those whose pattern of work is about to be disrupted, there is probably only one question that preoccupies them. 'So how does this shift affect my job, my team and my service?'

It's a totally legitimate and understandable question.

Within this response will be contained many different emotions and levels of personal interest. Some will want to know immediately how they will be affected. Any potential change in employment status could be significant positively and/or negatively. Some will want to know if their job is disappearing as the opportunity may bring the possibility of early retirement or starting projects only dreamed about. Many who have been in the same role for years will be worried about how to bring their CV up to date. Some will be concerned about the impact on the quality of the service they have spent years building with colleagues, or the impact on clients, customers and end users.

Change affects people's lives. It's not just about counting beans.

The challenge for leaders is that the specific question about whose job will go away, be outsourced, morphed into another role, offer promotion, be downgraded or stay the same, will often not be clear at the beginning of any change programme. So the legitimate question becomes a tricky one to handle although it must be tackled at some point nonetheless. Leaders have to learn the art of saying in the initial stages that they 'don't know' some things and then be able to run with the consequences of this necessarily opaque reply.

Three questions that have to be addressed

There are three other questions however which do demand an adequate answer from the start and will in part affect how leaders respond to the challenge of 'so what's going to happen to my job?' Those three questions are simply:

* Why are we doing this?

* Where are we trying to get to and what does this look like?

* How are we planning to get there?

In my book 'Ensuring change delivers success' (2017), I outline the five key phases of a change programme and the associated activities and decision points. It is my contention that the process will help to lead people practically through the challenges of the three questions above. The book describes a flow of choices whilst (hopefully) not falling into the trap of prescribing a 'one size fits all' solution or defining the perfect pathway. There isn't one.

In this book, the intention is to describe in breadth and some depth the foundational principles underpinning the three questions above because they are absolutely central to any intentional shift in practice. They hold together all the phases described in my earlier work and breath life into the 'end to end' process.

In our experience, some leaders do grasp the importance of being able to define 'why, where and how' but then get distracted by the 101 other things that need to be going on. Most senior leaders remind us that they have a business to run as well as delivering the change. This results in them often becoming unsighted particularly around the bigger picture. We also observe that some have a very limited understanding of the depth, beneath which are fundamental touch points. They use the language of navigation but not the principles or indeed the tools. Some leaders also just seem to freeze when they start to see the enormity of the journey in front of them.

So to restate, the aim of this book is either to remind you of, or to introduce you to, the principles of navigating in a complex and ever changing organisational or business context carefully, but exploiting, too, the opportunities that exist. These principles will lie at the heart of navigating all change, including Digital Transformation.

Interestingly the questions of 'why, where and how' mesh into the three fundamental constructs underpinning navigation:

* Where are we now? (which informs 'why change?').

* What is the intended destination? ('where are we trying to get to?').

* What does the journey look like and feature? ('how are we going to get there?').

These seem simple questions but it is in depth of experience that they can only be truly understood and answered.

An apprenticeship in navigation

As already mentioned, I suspect that over the next few decades more attention will go into and prominence will be afforded to the development, training and assessment of a leader's ability to navigate.

This will take time, as navigation is more than just the application of some rules or mathematical calculations. It uses judgement based on information from multiple and sometimes surprising sources. It weighs up competing actions, is brought to life through experience, and is given clarity and depth by often the pain of failure and reflective practice. In short it has to become the very fabric of how a leader makes choices in order to steer the vessel (business) he or she is responsible for. Future training has to start early, have robustness , and focus on practical application.

My work life started at sea as a deck hand on a passenger ferry. The owner of the company, Robert

Arthur Hale, was a self-made businessman and entrepreneur. Through gutsy hard work he had become a master shipwright. Eventually he built the first of what was to become a fleet of seven ferries that operated from the south coast of the UK. He had been trained as an apprentice and this educational model had a great impact on him. Before mentoring, coaching and personal development became the staple of business life, he was living it. It was part of his business DNA. His passion was looking out for raw potential in those he hired and then moulding and supporting people to grow, take risks and find out what they could actually do. As well as being my mentor, he became a close friend. He was also a great businessman. At times he was tough and awkward to deal with particularly if he didn't trust you. He also had a rare ability to be successful in a world governed by compliance and regulations and yet not lose sight of the fact that we worked in the leisure and service industry.

I was employed to do all the dirty jobs, which involved cleaning, keeping the bilges in good shape and managing the ropes. I threw myself into the work with enthusiasm. Over time Bob Hale taught me how to pilot, navigate, respond to emergencies, manage the various stakeholders and provide an excellent customer experience for the passengers who had paid to use our services. We also spent hours in shipyards where he taught me how ships were made. All of this experience became part of my leadership DNA.

When I became qualified as a captain with a class 6 certificate, (for vessels carrying up to 250 passengers) he expected me to coach and bring on my crew in the same way he habitually did. He didn't have succession plans but was committed to reproduce the things he believed in, in those he employed.

As part of my development I learnt, understood and could apply the Regulations for the Prevention of Collisions at Sea along with practical seamanship. I became a licensed radio operator, understood meteorology, the standards and legal requirements of operating ferries, and the skills and values to run a 'good ship'. As best I could, I also incorporated the wisdom that had been handed down by experience from those who had gone before. The oral tradition of stories featuring disasters and outrageous successes has served me well over the years.

When I took command for the very first time I had to begin to make all of this my own and bring it alive for my crew and me. We never lost sight of the importance of our fee-paying passengers who ultimately paid the bills and our wages.

The essence of navigation
Amongst all of the detail of specific compliance laws and regulations I learnt the importance of the three key principles that underpin good navigation and safe and successful passage:

- Knowing exactly where I was at any given moment and being able to express this in multiple ways. This included my exact location on the earth's surface, where we were in relation to weather fronts coming in at various times, fuel levels and rates of usage, operational effectiveness, competency and morale of the crew, provisions for the voyage, speed over the ground, and so on.

- Knowing where my intentional destination was. Here some emphasis is on the word 'intentional', recognising that this was subject to all kinds of factors that may not be in my control.

- A plan of the voyage showing way points and times when decisions had to be made based on known moments where 'if this happens, then we will do this', or 'in this circumstance we will do that'. Of course the voyage itself was also subject to all of the 'off plan' events that happen with the vagaries of life at sea. Seas and oceans and landmasses defined the boundaries so decision making was set against this wide seascape. I was seldom hemmed in by some narrow restrictive view of what was possible. In Digital Transformation terms this is an important point to make.

// Warren Bennis in his bestselling book on Becoming a Leader (1989) describes 'true leaders' as being those who are 'pregnant with ideas' and who want to make things happen.

So when I moved into business working for one of the world's largest computer corporations I was delighted to find that many of the constructs I had used at sea were being used in business. They were expressed in slightly different language but were essentially the same principles.

Navigation at the heart of leadership
There are several hundred thousand books on leadership, and they are being published at the rate of about four a day (laroc, 2015). What runs through most of them is that the leader's role is about moving forward, being at the front, finding a way through conflicting pulls and challenging terrains whilst ensuring all effort is

focused on getting everyone involved to the new place. Hopefully this 'new place' would be better or more secure than where they were before. It could also be a place to deliver cargo or passengers. Or of course it may just be a fascinating place to explore...

Leaders by and large want to make a difference and that generally means going somewhere. Warren Bennis in his best selling book 'On becoming a leader' (1989) describes 'true leaders' as being those who are 'pregnant with ideas' and who want to make things happen. This is in contrast with the 'pseudo leaders' who want the title, the car and the office, but have little to say that is of any importance.

The main feature of a journey towards some better destination is that that destination is always in the future. This statement of the rather obvious hides the fact that despite this, many people (and electorates) want leaders (and politicians) to be able to describe this future place with total accuracy and certainty. The truth is that much will be unknown at the start. In these extraordinary times our ability to say 'this is exactly how it will exactly look' is limited. At best we may have a lot of informative data, some interesting questions, an outline... that taken together creates a 'compelling glimpse'.

Leaders also have to deal with the real-time conditions of the present and some of those are brutal and demand tough but wise choices.

So both decision making and decision taking (see over for the distinction) define much of the work that goes on. At sea even in open water many adjustments on the wheel are made to hold to the course. Each change will be deliberate and intentional.

On the bridge as in the boardroom we will all be intimately involved in making choices on a continual basis. Some of these will be straightforward, others less so. The quality and speed of decisions is also a key factor in navigation. At sea you discover very quickly how your choices and decisions work out. I learnt early on that as captain I was required to be responsible for the consequences of these choices and the buck quite rightly stopped with me.

In some places where I have worked I notice that the leadership game can be to move to the next job or next role before having to take responsibility for previous choices and actions. This is such a dangerous pattern as organisations can end up being steered by people who are not very good and some should be, quite frankly, disqualified to lead. This is why I would like to see leaders judged on their navigational record, which will always consider outcomes as defined by independent evaluation.

I suspect we are very vulnerable at this time of massive change, as inexperienced navigators are bluffing their way into influential positions. At sea if I mess up I am investigated by an independent body and held to account. Many of the current batch of organisational offenders, who are well known, seem to be jumping ship just before they are found out; going to other roles, getting promotions and running special projects, and becoming advisers and chairs of this and that.

Can I suggest it is time to start holding irresponsible leaders to account and become less tolerant of the mess that they habitually leave behind.

Decision making is shaped by culture

I learned through my corporate experience that a quick way of figuring out how any organisation operated, including a good insight into the real culture, is to understand how decisions are taken and made. Just these two pieces of information tell you so much about the operation as well as the real vision and values as opposed to the published ones.

'Decision making' describes the process of gathering information for a decision that is to be taken. This includes calibrating the complexity, impact and risk of the issue. It may involve research, consultative work, and/or a participative approach where key stakeholders are involved; or it could involve a trade-off with those who are affected by the decision. For simple and straightforward decisions this will mostly result in a clear and obvious statement of what should be done, and a decision can be taken easily and quickly. For more complex situations this evaluative process will identify a number of key options with a clear understanding of comparative risk. Then a decision has to be taken.

So decision taking refers to the moment when all of the analysis and choices have been delivered. This too has a level of complexity in the real world. So questions like who takes the final decision (individual, group or the defined decision taking procedure, particularly in legal judgements), how is it taken, the speed of the decision taking, where it is taken and how it is recorded and so on, are all critical.

All of the above are influenced by the culture of the organisation that simply defines 'how things get done around here'. So it is possible for an organisation to work collaboratively during decision making but the final decision is taken by one person. It is also feasible that one person produces the evidence base for a decision with options and risks, but the taking of that decision lies with a committee who will have their own rules about how things are decided (majority voting, consensus, chair with the final say, etc.).

If either process is opaque or they bleed into one another, confusion arises, which is why I separate the two phases.

Leaders have to continually 'read' the internal and external environment both in the 'here and now' and also along various points of the time line. At sea I learnt to put together many strands of information, interpret them, check them and translate them into events that would be likely to happen in 30 minutes, in two hours, or in a day or two. Joining up and interpreting information, and then being able to engage an entire system to good effect, is a key skill.

Leaders create and shape culture but they are part of it, so it shapes them and their decision making as well. In terms of navigation this is an important and systemic relationship to understand. There needs to be a real fit with the culture, obviously, but the leader needs also to be able to bring a difference of perspective. The ability to think independently at first and then interdependently with others is crucial. Disruptive change is going to require leaders to think and behave differently on a whole variety of fronts including the ability to unfreeze cultural patterns and then recreate and embed new positive habits. This will be an important part of the emerging future role. So back to the start...

/// Can I suggest it is time to start holding irresponsible leaders to account and become less tolerant of the mess that they habitually leave behind.

Why the *need* for this book?

Over the past two decades we have supported leaders and leadership teams taking their organisations through change of varying sorts. Some have done this because they wanted to seize some future opportunity and some have been driven to it because the current reality was unsustainable. Often it was a mixture of both. The pressure on leaders is intense because with all change comes informal scrutiny given to those in 'point position'. So everyone has a view on how the leader is performing. The reality too is that along with the change there will be a business to run, or, in some situations, to run down.

We have seen many different responses over the years.

Some have risen to the challenge and done a simply stunning job of navigating through tricky waters, continually winning the debate around the three primary questions of 'why, where and how'. The emphasis here is on continually winning... it's not a one-off effort. Many, though, as already mentioned, have become distracted by 101 pulls from different directions,

sometimes becoming caught in the mesh of the political game playing that often goes on.

Some lose sight of those three basic questions and the whole effort feels like a bureaucratic exercise. As a result presentations are loaded with detail but not with meaning.

Some leaderships think they have dealt with these questions of 'why, where and how' at the start of the change and fail to remind people of what it is all about and encourage their hearts on a regular basis. As a result they lose their people's willing support. Communication needs to be in different forms using different platforms and continual.

Sadly there are what feels like an increasing number of leaders who have an inexact and shallow understanding of their role as 'helmsperson and navigator' and all that goes along with this. As a result we have seen far too many organisational leaders who are:

- convinced of their own rightness, ignoring other views and perceptions - the line between confidence and hubris is often very thin;

- convinced that not having a vision is okay and just wander around without intention and meaningful direction;

- confusing straplines with vision;

- in vessels under way but not under command;

- in vessels under way but making no progress;

- running aground on sandbanks that have shifted position since the last time the leadership went this way;

- not taking into account employees who are tired, stressed and whose goodwill is being stretched to breaking point;

- working with insufficient resources to finish the journey, partly because they were not accurately assessed at the start or funding has been removed or reduced half way into the change and there is no contingency;

- using out of date or single stream data to figure out the starting position; tied to out-dated practices and procedures;

- convinced that the best plan to move between two points is a straight line regardless of traffic, incoming weather fronts or obstacles just below the surface;

- not making full use of technology;

- and so on….

Considering the low success rate of change programmes, the points mentioned, along with a myriad of other issues, are having a significant impact on the UK performance and ability to shift when required. This is a time when business needs to be smart, agile and productive. The digital revolution has an enormous role to play in this and provides data, tools, processes and new invention.

So in short we are hearing the terms associated with navigation and change leadership… but we are not seeing, consistently, the depth of understanding that goes behind the terms.

Is this being too critical? The 15%-20 % success rate of realising intended performance gains, as recorded by the Atticus (n.d.) Change Ability research, would say not. Ross Harling's (2017) analysis of DT success is also sobering and should result in a call to action. My own first hand experience of trying to salvage change programmes over the last 30 years is haunting. Fundamentally something has to shift in our current approach.

The need for precision is a part of this shift

As a navigator I will be able to express direction in a number of ways, all with a different meaning.

I might be steering on a bearing, which is the direction of one object from another.

My course is the direction my vessel is intended to be steered.

My heading is the direction my vessel is actually going at a particular moment, which is very rarely the same as the course.

Course over ground is the direction the vessel is actually moving over the surface of the earth. By building in the effects of wind and tide this is not usually the same as heading.

Does any of this matter? To a navigator, yes. This is why I am uncomfortable with the current preference of many leaders to drop the term 'vision' and adopt the phrase 'direction of travel'. This to me seems to say: 'we just happen to be heading this way… so this is the way we are going'. This lack of intentional direction is, I suspect, at the heart of many issues facing some organisations. Certainly in every organisation that has adopted the term 'direction of travel' people complain about the lack of directional clarity.

Recently a client told me having explained the above that I was being semantic. This was from someone presiding over a change with a lack of meaningful vision or intention and chaos ruled. And that is the point. The precision of navigation requires me to be very clear and to be able to differentiate between various responses and actions. A vague grasp of navigation doesn't allow the leader to do this, and the result is always painful.

Back to the basics of change

Most organisations use the following model outlined in Figure 1 below to frame a change.

This is the basis of any gap analysis and the start of many change programmes. As a high-level picture it works well. The issues though start to arise if the understanding of basic navigational principles lacks depth and breadth of experience to bring the data and the model alive.

What follows in the next sections therefore is a summary of the key points associated with each of the foundational questions and principles underpinning navigation. I will illustrate what is involved, give some examples of current practice and provide some questions to explore.

This is a time which requires those leading change to have a real mastery of navigational principles and practices.

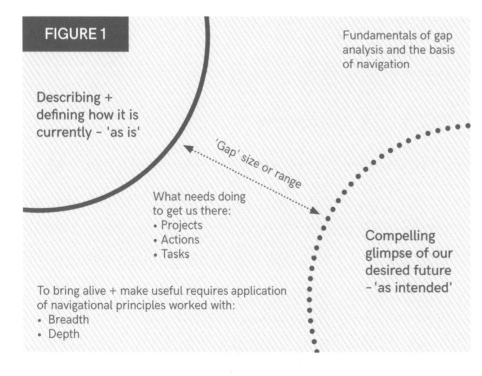

FIGURE 1

Fundamentals of gap analysis and the basis of navigation

Describing + defining how it is currently - 'as is'

'Gap' size or range

What needs doing to get us there:
- Projects
- Actions
- Tasks

Compelling glimpse of our desired future – 'as intended'

To bring alive + make useful requires application of navigational principles worked with:
- Breadth
- Depth

Navigational Principle 1

Where are we exactly? Figuring out current location and implications of this using multiple measures.

To the untrained person, it seems an easy task to express where you (or your organisation) exactly are. The reality however is very different. From our experience organisations frequently use too narrow a set of indicators – usually financial with sometimes a cultural perspective – to describe performance. Sometimes even these have not been prepared robustly enough. As a navigator I always use multiple points of reference and I drive out as much error as possible, because knowing where I am starting from and in what condition is so critical. This is what we will explore in more depth in this section.

F or many leaders figuring out where the organisation is in reality can be uncomfortable or even threatening. This is why even at the start point of the journey some courage is required.

Waymarks to navigate this section

Where are we? Defining the current location using multiple reference sites

One of the common issues of the simple gap analysis (Figure 1) is that it is often just the financial data that is taken seriously, with perhaps a cultural analysis on occasion. Although this is obviously really important information, it is too narrow a set of indicators to describe the richness and complexity of organisational life.

As a navigator I am required to know and be able to tell others where I am, with the precision required by my situation, at any specific time.

This assessment is always made because it informs decisions about the future journey. This is an important point to emphasise.

At sea we rely on some time-honoured equipment and some basic mathematics along with an incredible array of electronic and IT tools and applications. We use multiple sources, some to triangulate data (as we know some degree of error exists in our tools and through our usage) and some to be able to express where we are in relation to a variety of other disciplines and lines of information.

Along with the stunning technology, I am obliged to have a permanent (human) lookout. Literally these 'pair of eyes' that continually scan both near positions and the horizon, are critical. The skill is being able to identify and interpret both obvious and more subtle happenings around the vessel. I describe this ability as being able to 'read' what's going on. A very experienced captain described it to me as 'letting your eyes continually do the work'.

At the time of writing the US navy have recently experienced a number of serious collisions in the Pacific with tragic loss of life. The destroyer USS Fitzgerald struck a commercial ship in the waters off Japan killing seven US sailors. The destroyer USS John McCain collided with an oil tanker in coastal waters off Singapore in August 2017 killing 10 US sailors. Five officers involved in these incidents have been charged with negligent homicide.

This is a tragedy on so many levels and most former mariners will have great sympathy for families and crew. The tough question within the heartache is how is it that warships brimming with the very latest technology, including systems that use artificial Intelligence, can collide with very large, relatively slow moving and very visible commercial vessels?

The US navy has just released summaries of what it has found out and this is reported in The Diplomat with a piece written by Stephen Stashwick on 20 November 2017 concerning the USS John McCain. The article gives a full account of the events and decisions leading up to the collision. In summary it appears that the ship was approaching a very busy shipping lane equipped with a traffic separation scheme, with a strong tide running. The captain decided that it was more important to give sailors rest time before entering port rather than have a full compliment of watches on the bridge. This decision was taken against the advice of senior colleagues. The helmsman, manually steering the ship, had difficulties staying on course at the right speed. The captain ordered the throttle control be transferred to another system leaving the helmsman to focus on steering. Unfortunately steering control was also transferred but this was not spotted. The helmsman reported a loss of steering control. Over a period of two minutes the steering control was shifted to various locations. Confusion followed. This was all then compounded when an order to reduce speed resulted in just the port engine slowing to 5 knots whilst the starboard side engine remained at a speed of 20 knots, which effectively pushed the ship to port. This veering to the left was made worse by the strong currents and apparent loss of steering. The helmsman believed that the two throttles controlling the propeller shafts were linked into one system. They weren't.

There may be an issue with the design of the instrumentation as well as the training in its use. It appears also that the physical throttles had been replaced by a digital screen interface controlled with a keyboard and trackball. The helmsman ended up chasing the curser around the screen. Human error and confusion, compounded by mistakes that grew in systemic impact, lack of training and poor control design seem to be at the heart of this tragedy.

Within this story is contained the elements and patterns that make up many disasters both at sea and in our marketplaces. In business and in the government sectors I suspect that with the advancement of Digital Transformation, the equivalent of this story will become even more common. The reason I say this is that I don't think we have a handle yet on the implications and impact of AI and repetitive automated processes, and speed is critical. Two minutes on the USS Jonn S. McCain was the window available to correct things and

it closed very fast as it always does at sea. Technology works at a speed beyond human capacity so if it is both learning and making decisions we need to figure out potential problems before a major incident occurs. In response to these naval incidents and fears over security the US navy has reinstated training for all officer cadets in the use of the sextant as a navigational instrument and the use of compass and pencils. Technology on the bridge is extensive, however it is also potentially vulnerable to cyber attack which could render a ship effectively 'dead in the water'. As an insurance policy US naval command have decided that their navigators need to learn how to use some old technology... just in case. More than that it also embeds the principles that underpin the technology and enable the data to be interpreted intelligently. This is a good example of the principles of navigation, in this case principle 1, transcending the tools and digital capability.

Technology is critical in producing data – the question as always is 'what is the data telling us'?

This situation has great resonance with trends in many businesses that require more from less. Whilst 'working smarter' is perfectly sensible, there are limits. In the case of the US navy this may have caused many lives to needlessly be lost.

So back to answering the question of 'where am I?'

> As a navigator I am required to know and be able to tell others where I am, with the precision required by my situation, at any specific time.

An answer using multiple points of reference

I will be able to give a grid reference of an exact location, I will be able to say how much ground we are covering (tides and winds require a more sophisticated answer than simple speed). I will be able to describe our heading, bearing and course. (Although these terms sound as if they are describing the same thing they are in fact distinct, as we saw earlier). I will be able to say how much fuel we have; how many gallons or tonnes are being used per hour; the state of vital provisions; the readiness of the crew in relation to (a) normal running conditions and (b) emergency situations; where we are in relation to other moving vessels and incoming weather fronts; ... and the list could go on.

The answer involves multiple assessments of many factors – which is why the question of 'where am I?' is more complex and requires a fuller explanation. And (to repeat) this is all-important because it informs what needs to happen next on our passage and journey. It's not information for information sake.

In business we are exposed to increasing risk by answering the 'Where am I' question within narrow parameters that ignore rather important other elements. Take for example mergers and acquisitions (M&As). Due diligence, which all would agree is critically important, in reality only measures a fairly restricted view of a company's health. This measure is very important but it is not the only one that counts.

Despite all of the attention of lawyers and accountants the success rate of M&As is low. Roger Martin (2016) states in the Harvard Business Review that 70-90% of M&As fail to deliver real advantage. It strikes me that along with an examination of the books, some more scrutiny needs to be put in place to understand cultural fit, change readiness and the current state of digital platforms, processes and capability – to broaden by just a few elements, and there are many more.

Here are just two examples of why this is important:

When Hewlett Packard bought Compaq Computers very little attention was given to their two very different cultural ways of operating. Compaq had a culture that said 'better to make a wrong decision than a slow one'. So 'shoot, draw, aim'. HP, being more 'West Coast', involved many personnel in decision making and always tried to reach agreement by consensus. 'Better to make the right decision first time around than a fast one that is poor'. When these giants were brought together, the confusion was significant and was particularly observable around decision making. The Vice President I worked for was immensely frustrated as these two cultures collided and struggled for supremacy. The ensuing mess had real impact on her worldwide business operation by immobilising business decision taking. This in turn hurt the customer and HP. The company eventually resolved the issue through a process called 'adopt and go'. This meant that those who were affected by, any decision (or part of it), could debate and argue, but once a decision had been taken, the effort shifted to implementation. At this point no one could drive the process back into more debate.

A local council in the UK wanted to outsource the IT department to save money. The leaders ignored the pleas of the workforce to understand in more depth and breadth, what the department actually did rather than what was on paper. When sold off, the new outsourcing company started charging for what they saw as all of the additional work that was outside of scope and contract.

Soon the savings that were supposed to be achieved by this change were looking very thin. This was all because the leadership refused to conduct an analysis of workflows and processes in the real world and relied on the service plans that existed but that were hopelessly out of date.

The cost of change

We see many examples in the UK where a basic gap analysis has been completed and the decision to change has been made but without a fully considered picture of the current reality. A consequence of this is that despite some of the associated costs and systemic implications being obvious many more will be hidden in parts of the operation that are 'off radar' or not joined up. If the diagnostics have not been done thoroughly then these invisible costs and consequences will begin to bubble to the surface downstream of the original decisions. Consequently by the time they do appear, the cost tag will have risen in many cases.

A good friend was a therapist in the NHS and was part of a fully integrated team of specialists. Historically her department had gone through many changes and reorganisations and although there were some inadequacies of resource, the goodwill of the teams had made things work despite the shortcomings of whatever change programme was happening at the time. But every inefficient transformation programme that had gone before had a price tag. The real cost was the morale of a high-performing team.

In the latest merger with an underperforming NHS Trust, the 'cost' was loaded still further on the teams. They were expected to do 'impossible' jobs, have their pay grade rescheduled backwards and compromise on the quality of care offered to families in the community. Of course this was all subject to a consultation…. The final blow came when they found out that all the decisions had already been taken and the 'consultation' was merely to comply with protocol. The profound disappointment from learning that they had been misled (presumably intentionally) resulted in the majority of the experienced and senior front line staff leaving the profession.

Today there is little developmental and therapeutic provision in this region of the UK. Because the Trust no longer has the capability or capacity in house to deliver what they are legally mandated to provide, they have to go to the contracts market. Such contractors will not have the experience both professionally (using less experienced staff means a perceived lower cost) and won't be locally connected with other support services. It would also be an interesting exercise to do the maths on all of this, as contracting out when viewed as whole is often more expensive than keeping things in house. Of course, this is a hot political debate in both central and local government as well as the NHS.

In short a poorer service for probably more money.

Someone should have had the wit to find out the current levels of change fatigue within the service as well as listen to their solutions to meet a challenging future – and they did have some. This then should have been assessed against the risk of losing swathes of professional and managerial experience. A more supportive way of approaching the change might have meant that the Health Trust retained its professionals and families retained the hope of better life outcomes. And of course it would have been cheaper.

The approach adopted however, seems to many to represent utter stupidity.

Best practice requires leadership to put all data together and understand the current state from multiple standpoints.

To do this, systems need to be intelligently integrated and for there to be a high degree of openness and trust between services, and departments that make up the overall system. As Patrick Lencioni (2002) asserts, trust is everything.

> If the diagnostics have not been done thoroughly then these invisible costs and consequences will begin to bubble to the surface downstream of the original decisions

A lack of trust limits information flow

Low levels of trust result in either a reduction of information shared, or the possibility of infighting between functions and departments where information is intentionally withheld to bolster power bases. All of this limits vital information flow and seriously impacts the ability to define the current position. This in turn starts to affect future choices and decisions negatively.

In systems and organisations that have any degree of complexity, information and data held by two separate groups might only be understood fully when they are brought together in the public domain. If there is little sharing or wider scrutiny they might remain just two disconnected bits of data.

Understanding the full 'end to end' process is therefore vital. For leaders this means creating a culture of trust and making sure little is hidden off the radar. Where there is a lack of real sharing, the result can be a prolonged dispute about what the exact 'current reality looks like'. This in turn, delays action. It is at this point another 'incident at sea' begins to slowly unfold. Incidents can very quickly turn into disasters.

In fact some politically orientated organisations use this problem as a device to avoid doing anything substantial and use 'further research', or 'further analysis' to kick the ball into the long grass. I could name some institutions that have elevated the practice into an art form.

In the introduction to this section I used a specific description of using the 'precision required by the situation'. This is a nautical principle that states you need enough information to make the decision, given what is going on in the real world. Both under-analysis and over-analysis carry risks of their own.

One large organisation spent 18 months arguing amongst the service heads about whose view of the current state was the most accurate. During this time and despite all of the effort to 'transform', nothing much changed and the enterprise went into decline. At sea this is termed as 'being under way, not under command and not making way' and puts at risk the ship, the crew and the passengers. It has all the ingredients of a tragedy about to happen.

An issue facing many organisations is a lack of a systemic view of the whole enterprise and the role Digital Transformation can play. Often processes are not linked up and very few if any of the leaders have a handle on the 'end to end' workflows. The issue is further compounded when trust is low, since information is, as already mentioned, either intentionally or unwittingly withheld. This will always impact the quality and timing of various choices that have to be made during a change by the leadership. Making the right choices at the right time is what navigation is all about.

In business as well as at sea fixing a current location and being able to describe it to the wider world as it really is and not how some think it should be, is critical.

An assumption of error and important adjustments

If I want to establish my exact position as a grid reference, I have little to do: my GPS will have automatically worked this out. In fact at present I can get an exact readout continually so long as the US continues to allow access to its satellites. Before the advent of this technology I had to rely on compass, chart and or sextant, along with some basic sums and specific information.

If I was in sight of land I would take a compass bearing on a known feature, translate magnetic bearings into those used on my chart that relate to 'true north', work out the back bearing and draw a line on my chart from the feature out to sea. This single point of reference in essence told me I was somewhere near this line and somewhere along its length. So a start had been made, but this had limited use. What was needed was a cross-reference. I would therefore find another known point and repeat the process. This would give a point of intersection where the two lines meet, as shown in Figure 2.

In theory this should be my position... but of course it rarely is – if ever.

At sea we assume error will have occurred. For example the compass being used will have been affected by all of the electrical equipment and will be giving a marginal but false reading. As captain I am responsible each year to discover the extent of this error and compensate for it in all calculations. This known 'deviation' is then incorporated into my workings.

The variation between magnetic north and true north is also added or subtracted depending on whether I am working from compass to chart or from chart to compass, with the extent of the variation being dictated by where I am on the planet.

In 2003 the earth's magnetic pole was 900 km away from the real North Pole so the calculations to account for this variation would use different figures in Alaska, in Denmark and around the coast of the UK. And just to make life interesting (!) this figure changes from year to year, although this westerly figure (for us in the UK) is declining at a predictable rate. My maths takes all this into account.

However in highlighting some of the complexity all I am trying to illustrate is that error has many places to creep in. Even in simple tasks like taking a compass bearing on a visible landmark I may not have had an exact fix on the known feature and the reading could be out by a half a degree or more. Over a distance this becomes increasingly significant.

Now we try to be as accurate as we can at every stage... but just to nail our position we opt for a third compass bearing on another known feature and do the maths and then draw a third line on a chart. This gives us a triangulation and is called the 'triangle of error' or the 'cocked hat'. So it appears on the chart as a little triangle at the intersection of three lines (Figure 3). With some confidence we can now say we are located somewhere close to this 'triangle of error'.

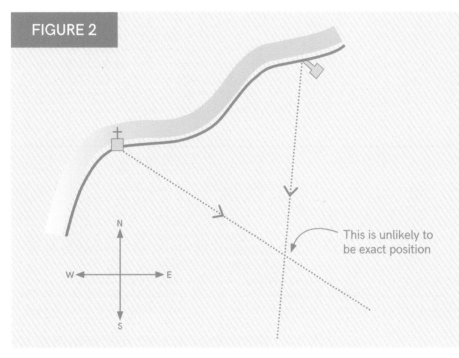

FIGURE 2

This is unlikely to be exact position

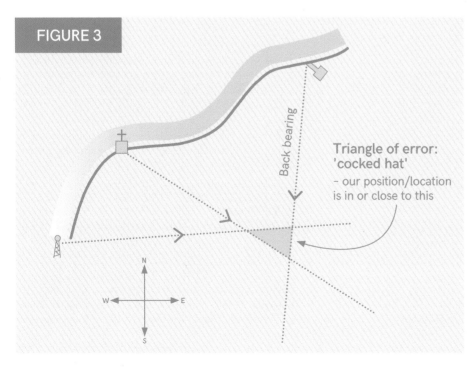

FIGURE 3

Back bearing

Triangle of error: 'cocked hat'
– our position/location is in or close to this

Navigators at times have to be 'glass half-empty' people, so even with a triangle of error identified we would instinctively place ourselves, even in this small area, closest to any potential danger. This is borne out by the maths that give just a 25% chance of the exact location still being in the cocked hat.

GPS and satellite location works in the exact same way but with the extent of the errors being amazingly small, providing greater confidence that our grid reference is indeed very close to our actual position. This is critical if we want to be found quickly for whatever reason and it gives the start place for the on-going voyage.

/// In reality too much time is spent trying to retrofit solutions into inadequately understood starting positions that have been the result of poor diagnostics.

The relevance to organisations

Like any vessel, a business needs to know its current location before attempting any change. However the time needed and the real cost, as well as inadequate tools and sampling strategy, result in some pretty flimsy diagnostic work at times. This might be fine if there is little risk of errors and the change is not complex. The reality is often very different.

A reluctance to take time and invest money

When we put out proposals to support our customers through change, including a full set of costs detailing the diagnostic plan, it is this that is most often challenged. Some of our customers view it as just a cost with no real value. Consultants work in a competitive industry too, so we will always look at ways to make things affordable but we never compromise on the thoroughness of the diagnostic work. It is just too important. No one would want to go through a medical operation based on inadequate evaluation before hand. Businesses should be no different.

In reality too much time is spent trying to retrofit solutions into inadequately understood starting positions that have been the result of poor diagnostics. Here is an example:

"Flexible working is just about reducing costs." (If you are prepared to pay the investment cost first...)

I once challenged a politician who was responsible for implementing a flexible working arrangement across an

entire local council in order to drive down operating expenditure. Just to be very open, I really am a supporter of flexible working and along with colleagues from Digital, 3M and Xerox did much of the early pioneering work some 30 years ago to explore this concept.

However as part of the return-on-investment (ROI) calculation you do need to have figured out the cost of implementation.

So my simple question to the politician was how much was the shift to flexible working going to cost? He said I didn't understand and the effort was all about cost cutting. I said I did get this, but my question was still the same. He became flustered and started to bluster his way out of what was an increasingly uncomfortable conversation. So I got specific:

* What was the cost of buying everyone who needed it a decent laptop and appropriate operating systems with current security software?

* What were the 'back up' costs?

* What were the on-going costs of training people how to use the technology and associated tools?

* What were the associated costs of creating space for employees to work on sensitive personal information given that they were not legally allowed to take this data out of the office and off site?

* What was the estimated cost of room hire for team meetings?

He responded to the latter point, 'people could meet in coffee shops' to which I responded 'are you seriously wanting political, personal and operationally sensitive conversations taking place in the public domain with the likelihood of it being overheard?

And so it went on. The politician had no answers to these simple questions and no clue why they were important. Chaos ensued during implementation…. It was bound to. There were no other likely outcomes.

Despite the excuse of 'hindsight is a wonderful teacher' being rolled out post-programme, the failure arose from not looking forward intelligently. And anyway few people really learn from hindsight, which is why history repeats itself.

Calibrating the tool

As mentioned, as a captain I am responsible every year for an activity called 'swinging the compass'. Briefly, this is a calibration exercise to flush out the current error that has been caused by the proximity of my ship's compass to other magnetic sources causing distortion and a slight loss of accuracy. This figure is the 'deviation' that I apply to all workings.

The tools we use in organisational diagnostics also need scrutiny and calibration.

A few years ago we were asked to help a police force get to the bottom of why poor morale was persisting amongst the non-uniformed part of the force. They had tried many things to fix the issue over the years and nothing had worked. They rightly felt they were missing something….

It was very clear that morale was at rock bottom and most people were pretty grumpy. In fact many seemed very angry. The staff survey that was conducted every six months to monitor how employees were feeling, continually commented on this. The results all indicated that over the years the situation had continued to deteriorate and was now critical.

We set up a structured engagement process we have designed called the 'diagnostic hub'. In simple terms these are multiple sets of conversations that are of real interest to employees and deploy the navigational principle of collecting information from many different viewpoints. We reached about 80% of the community using 8 diagnostic subjects. The core finding was that the staff survey was itself responsible for much of the poor morale.

Issued every six months it asked the same questions over and over. Because of the amount of data produced each time, the results weren't published before the next survey was due. So everyone on the arrival of the latest survey sunk deeper into frustration, anger and cynicism. This was further amplified by the fact that no one ever did anything about providing answers to the questions that were being raised. Same questions asked over and over, plus no answers and no change was a sure-fire way of turning the most optimistic people very cynical.

We recommended suspending the survey for a year or two and just talking to people.

When an organisation asks 'where are we'?, who is the 'we'?
What adds complexity to answering this first question of navigation is the size, spread and divisional structure of the enterprise. The 'we' needs defining.

Large corporates may need to be able to answer the question on the basis of geographic region or country and/or function. Some local authorities in the UK may need to start by answering in terms of individual services. So the answer could be complex. In a large international corporation, one region might be doing very well and

others not so well. So if the change were to encompass all of the business, the variance would need to be acknowledged and built into the overall analysis.

In one council in the UK, all of the services were pretty poor and in various states of brokenness. The organisation was close to going into special measures. The exception was the Education Authority. This was outstanding and a role model for other authorities. So the diagnostic work had to be uncompromising in its search for truths, but it was critical too not to lose sight of the fact that within the toxicity was a centre of excellence.

This proved a tricky one to handle for members and officers. But to their credit they got the final statements exactly right as to why it was imperative to change, whilst upholding the reputation of a first-class service. They managed not to 'tick people off' by constantly referring to how good education was and how much everyone else needed to learn from it. If this had been the message, future collaboration would have been minimal as the majority of the other services became 'sick to death' hearing about it. The leaders worked with great humility and some wisdom. This was only achieved because the CEO and the elected leader of the council had the courage to tackle issues of their relationship head on.

> **// It takes courage and some awareness to confront how things really are rather than how you'd like them to be.**

Facing the uncomfortable reality at times
Jim Collins (2001) reminded us all of a core business (and indeed life) principle called the 'Stockdale paradox'. This refers to the lessons learnt by Admiral Jim Stockdale, who as a prisoner of war in Vietnam was tortured 20 times during an 8-year imprisonment but despite everything came through with hope. Collins (quoting Stockdale) said 'you must never confuse faith, that will prevail in the end – which you can never afford to lose – with the discipline to confront the most brutal facts of your current reality, whatever they might be'.

It takes courage and some awareness to confront how things really are rather than how you would like them to be.

When B&Q in 2005 saw some of its rivals cease to trade I guess that it also saw the opportunity created by a shrinking market supply. However it was savvy enough to realise that the conditions its competitors were facing and struggling with, were the same ones that could take B&Q itself under. Rising costs, a falling footfall, a drop in like-for-like sales, customers who were increasingly differentiated in their need and the turbulence of international supply chains were some of the conditions threatening its future. Its response was to tackle each element head on. It did not shy away from some uncomfortable truths, which is why it is still trading. However the latest 'like for like' sales figures (Telegraph, 21 November 2017) show an overall decline of 5%, which should remind all of us in business that success and failure are never far apart. Navigation is a continual process not a one-off event.

Even if the reality is closure – how to finish well

The brutal reality of a closure with little hope of reprieve was the situation facing a European pharmaceutical company. Its UK operation was scheduled to close within 18 months. Because of the nature of the industry it had to keep operating with a standard of excellence and absolute attention to detail until the day came for it to literally 'switch off the lights'. This was to be the last act of the last manager through the door.

This proved to be one of the most remarkable stories I have seen in business.

The reality was closure, but the company decided that it was going to support its workforce throughout with many practical measures. It was determined to live by its values right up until the end. Of course there was concern, tears and fear for the future but by staying true to each other and what they all believed in, the 18 months became a story of overcoming and of personal triumph. It was both humbling and a privilege to see how, given support, people can come through. By the time the lights had been switched off, all the employees had found jobs, or started their own companies and/or taken early retirement. Everyone, too, could tell a remarkable story of how they all came through tough times by staying close to each other but in a way that no one expected when the closure news was first announced.

Supporting people

The example I have just outlined was quite extraordinary but it should also remind all leaders of the need to actively support employees and customers going through change, regardless of intended outcome. This support needs to be customised and specific.

There will be many reactions to changes and these will be amplified or suppressed by both the operating culture and personal styles, which will also be impacted by where people are located on what is commonly referred to as the 'transition curve'. So the same question of 'where are we', when applied to the people, also has to be specific and informed by multiple perspectives.

As part of figuring out where you are, all of this information, which shifts also over time, is critical. Where change is brought about while intelligently offering the right levels of support and challenge, people come through with fewer traumas and make the shifts faster; and, I would assert, the programme normally costs less.

In my experience macho cultures that see support as an inconvenient and additional cost, and employees as expendable if they don't shape up, normally pay a high price in so many ways. Rehiring for lost positions and filling capability gaps, retrofitting solutions, having to take an extended pause to find more money or clear up a mess resulting in a reduction of momentum, restructuring... and the list could go on – all of this because 'to support' is regarded as a sign of weakness.

When more intelligent enterprises define the current position, they include a prediction of what people might be feeling along the time line and determine specific actions to help those people through. A simple tool like the transition curve is a great way of figuring out what to do when, including when to focus on education and when to shift to training. Many organisations get the timing of these two very different approaches muddled up. Using Kubler-Ross's (1970) work describing the shift in the way people feel in terms of confidence and competence during the duration of a transition also clarifies what specific support is needed in the four main phases. These phases are termed denial, turbulence, exploration and commitment. Again it is important for leaders to get this right.

Then all of this is translated to teams and individuals. So the practical needs of those whose style is more 'Driver' like will be very different to those who are more 'Amiable'. 'Expressive' and 'Analytical' preferences will also require different strategies of support. The point is that support has to be targeted to the precise need of the situation and the different needs of people going through these times. This is why the team leader role is so important as it is here things are translated and given precision.

The good news is that most of this is entirely foreseeable and can be articulated as part of the 'where are we?' question before the impact of the change is felt. This work does not need to cost much either and certainly costs a lot less than mopping up mess and trying to retrofit solutions and apply patches.

A missing tool set?

As I 'scan the waters' around business looking at trends, and blips on the radar that are close and some appearing as faint shapes on the horizon, I am seeing some patterns emerging that we should take note of.

Many of the pioneers and visionaries of Digital Transformation are predicting disruptive change continuing in business and society in general. Old ways and old ideas will be confronted… that is not to say they will all be abandoned but they will be challenged at least. We know enough already to understand that our world will be very different as wave upon wave of increasingly intelligent technology ushers in opportunity and choices. At this present time we are clearly in a place of transition.

Tech companies that are genuinely excited about new capability are also guilty of overselling the results of sometimes untried and untested solutions. However when offered a 25-30% overall cost reduction, (which seems to be the figure being touted) organisations who are under enormous pressure to reduce costs are buying the claims without much critical review.

One council was so confident that the savings afforded by digitalisation were there for the taking, that it laid off a significant percentage of its workforce before implementing the digital solution. The solution did not deliver. The local authority later found out it was being used as a beta site for the vendor. Chaos ensued which meant the authority had to throw a great deal of money at patching things over and retrofitting systems and protocols in order to keep delivering for its users. Having worked for a tech corporation I know that when you have to start patching the patches, you have seriously lost control.

So we know Digital Transformation offers great opportunities but we need to be much more informed and savvy if we are to fully leverage future uplifts. Going back to the basics of Navigational Principle 1, we need very urgently to develop some tools and architectural principles that will allow us all to assess the state of a number of critical factors including change readiness and 'digital ability' as one of my colleagues has called it.

Currently assessment of an organisation's 'digital location' is not well informed and some choices are being made either in desperation or for political reasons that are having a far reaching impact. We need to get some sanity in to the situation fast. In Ross Harling's (2017a) article 'Will your council be a digital dynamo or dinosaur?' he begins to identify some of the traps and sets out some of the principles and tools that are required in this emergent area.

A significant and focused effort also needs to be made to help develop the 'reading ability' of those leaders working off-chart. According to friends working at the sharp end of the Digital Transformation, many leaders have good data but don't understand what the information is saying. They don't seem to grasp the questions they should be asking. Just to restate, the current success and failure statistics are indicating that we are very far from where we need to be if we are to realise the potential offered by 'new ways and new ideas'.

Summary

Figuring where you are, as precisely as is required, is critical but it is not always straightforward, particularly in organisations with any degree of complexity.
It takes courage and a willingness to face up to the reality of what is going on rather than hearing the siren voices echoing around in whatever bubble we are living in.

Multiple sourcing, gathering data from IT, operations, marketing, finance, legal, HR, and OD departments, and from customer sources, using tools like work and process mapping, change readiness assessment and cultural assessment as well as the traditional health indicators, are all imperatives. Smart organisations of course have much of this information at hand if they are up to date with the analytics. This does take time and money and needs to be calculated as part of the ROI.

Intelligent organisations know that there must be an assumption of error and triangulate to drive this out as much as is possible. All of this can be completed relatively quickly if there is will and resource - and of course, trust.

The bottom line of Navigational Principle 1 is that before any shift of position you should know where you are currently across multiple platforms and perspectives. All of this information when viewed together must answer the simple question. Why are we changing?

Some questions

- Does your organisation know where it is on a range of meaningful dimensions? This should include data from Finance, HR, IT, Legal, Customers, OD and L&D, Operations, Sales, Marketing and External Benchmarks.

- Who holds and has access to this information?

- Is the information visually displayed in clear and accessible terms?

- What kind of agreement exists that supports this assessment?

- Has the assessment been tested by a competent external source?

- Are the diagnostic tools calibrated sufficiently?

- Are these findings representing the whole enterprise/ system?

- What methods do you use to listen to the voices outside of the leadership bubble?

- How have you assessed your digital position?

- Have you both allowed for error of the diagnostic tool and triangulated your position?

- How is all of this affecting and informing how decisions are made and taken?

- Would the above question be answered in the same way throughout the organisation? How do you know?

- How robustly has cost been estimated and what are the contingency costs – just in case?

- Are the levels of relational trust sufficient given the demands of the change process?

Bringing together the key themes of this section and concluding insights

So the simple statement at the end of this substantive work, which will hopefully win the argument as to why change is going to happen, will sound something like... 'This is where we are and this is the reason we need to change. If we don't then this is what we will face but if we do, this is what we hope and anticipate'.

This may not necessarily be an uplifting message in itself, although it can bring clarity and surprising relief in some situations as it suggests that the situation is understood and something is about to be done. This will resonate further if the argument as to 'why the change' has been won sufficiently and with enough people.

Using a nautical metaphor, the ship has been untied from the dockside. We are about to start a voyage and are positioned to move away from the familiarity and patterns of what will quickly become 'the past'. The instruction to 'let go' and move away has to be compelling. It will probably be felt as a 'push' away from the present state. At this point as a leader you are trying to win people's understanding and influence their thinking.

The uplift and attraction comes from the next phase (Navigational Principle 2). This presents the hope arising from a picture of the future that is also compelling. It is about the vision outworked through a well thought through strategy.

Navigational Principle 2

Where do we intend to get to? Defining the hope with clarity, conviction and confidence that the disruption is worth it.

Vison can be described as a compelling glimpse of a desired future. It describes hope and it always provides the pulling momentum towards a better place ahead. However it is also a term that has become overused, or rather misused, over the recent years. A growing number of leaders refuse to use the terminology and provide less contentious descriptions such as 'direction of travel'.

Waymarks to navigate this section

Some leaders and their teams simply don't appear to have any meaningful vision. Where it does have its rightful place as the second navigational principle, wonderful things can still happen.

Vision Is...

There seems to be part of the human psyche that dreams about the time ahead. As we peer through the fog of possibilities, hope kicks in for a better or more secure future for ourselves, for our families, our communities, our countries and indeed our species. We have been curious over the ages to see what is over the next hill, the next mountain range, around the next bend in the river, and over the horizon. Whether driven by need or curiosity the human spirit is restless to 'see'. Sometimes seeing ahead is about the next few weeks, months or years. Then there are the rare individuals who combine creativity with imagination and picture a future beyond their own lives.

Landscape designers like Capability Brown shaped the countryside with the next few centuries in mind. I am still amazed by their skill and incredible ability to picture a mature landscape, as it would be seen by the generations to follow. I admire too people like Ken Olsen who worked in his garage near Boston to build one of the early and ground-breaking mainframe computers. Then there is the current and simply stunning work of Professor Miguel Nicolelis, pioneer of biomedical engineering who is transforming both robotics and brain therapy. The examples of course are endless... and I am sure each one of us has our own examples of how this person or that product or application has had a vision ahead of its time.

However the stuff of vision should not just be understood in third party terms. Just as vital is that it must speak of what you and I see for our futures. In business and organisational life it feels as though far too often vision can lack personal ownership, being talked about from afar. This is why when people do speak from head and heart and from their values, it causes others to take note. It feels authentic.

Some dream about social justice. Many young people dream of simply owning a home of their own. For far too many people globally, the dream is just a hope for food, clean water and a safe place to sleep. I have seen poverty and I am amazed at how resilient people can be and ashamed that they have to be that tough. Still, though, I am stunned at the capacity of people, despite all, to look forward... to imagine and to hope. Looking to the future seems to be part of our DNA.

Vision is a living, dynamic and meaningful picture of a future place. It always represents hope and if important enough will result in effort, time and money being invested to get to this place.

Vision also incudes what we are seeing on the journey, so that it can be defined and understood as a continual scanning of all that is going on around us. If we want to see positive and successfully implemented change, vision has to take centre stage.

For those who are weary of hearing the term – and I do understand the over use and hype that has gone with it over the past decades – I would simply ask that we remember its place as a core navigational principle. It also should not be watered down to fit some political expediency or correctness as some are currently doing. It is towards the vision and the intended destination that we set our course and it is this, that has the potential power to transform people and situations.

My mentor frequently asked me 'so what do you see...?' This question was posed not only when there was a lot going on but also in times where it seemed not much was happening. The years have taught me both were of importance and contained challenges and opportunities that might not be initially visible. Over time I began to grasp the depth, richness and wisdom that lay behind what appeared to be a very simple question. Without vision we shrivel and die, but with it we have hope and meaning; and in the simplest of terms... a future.

What I hope has become obvious in the previous section exploring Navigational Principle 1 is that in answering the question 'where are we?' leaders have to deal with many layers, complexities and nuances. Put bluntly, in order to successfully understand the current position you have to make the effort to understand the location of the entire system as it really is and not how we would like it to appear.

Navigational Principle 2 defines 'what we see' as our potential future and is equally as nuanced as Principle 1. It also provides many traps for the unwary.

The 'compelling glimpse' should galvanise and focus the efforts of leaders and leadership teams who are steering the enterprise, so that they will be prepared to go through whatever the conditions throw at them, to get to their intended destination. The word 'intention' can feel a bit too casual but that is not how a navigator would interpret it. It says there may be events outside of our control that could affect where we are trying to get to, but all effort is going to be made to arrive where we should, on time and within budget with the goodwill of the crew intact.

This future 'compelling place' must exist as a picture in our thoughts and imagination and has to be tangible enough to be described. Of course it will probably be described in various ways as the background culture, and the stylistic preferences of the person holding the vision kicks in, but it is this that enables us to set our course.

Making the vision as clear as you can about the intended place we are all going towards is just so critical to navigation. In fact I would assert that it is the whole point of any journey of change.

> Vision is a living, dynamic and meaningful picture of a future place. It always represents hope and if important enough will result in effort, time and money being invested to get to this place.

Common issues

I see three current and common abuses of Principle 2 in business life:

1 The principle can be overhyped so that any discussion about vision seems set in a galaxy far, far away. Vision can equally be presented in very uninspiring terms or in a mechanistic manner that lacks any real spark of life. In some organisations the term itself is all but banned. 'Direction of travel' or phrases like 'we are heading towards' are the replacement terms but tend to rob stakeholders of a sense of worthy destination and purpose. A positive vision of the future is replaced with functional plans, projects, goals and financial targets. These are all important but can feel a bit dry. Vision has the habit of disturbing patterns and the status quo and therefore can be a dangerous thing... that is why some avoid speaking of it.

2 Another abuse is an interpretation that says vision is always about bigger, faster, more powerful and more 'glitzy'. Sometimes in order to survive or indeed flourish in a new market or context we have to reduce or pull back from the demands of a previous vision and consolidate

or refocus. The hedgehog principle expounded by Isaiah Berlin (see Collins, 2015, pp.90-91) is the interface between what a company is best at, where the economics work well and what ignites the passion of the people. Sometimes this involves going back to the fundamentals the business was established on.

3 IT vendors can set exaggerated expectations about what their technologies can do. Their genuinely exciting picture of the future is often immature and untested. Desperate, mesmerised and unprepared customers are unfortunately willing to buy it. Thus wildly over-hyped claims from tech companies meeting desperate and naïve customer expectation is a disaster that is already happening on a regular basis.

What vision provides

When a 'compelling glimpse of a desired future' provides hope, fosters a strong desire for change with the right mix of the inspirational and the pragmatic, uses technology as the enabler, and sets out values that provide both consistency and glue, then great things can happen.

Vision has both a simplicity and complexity that competent leaderships understand and use fully in their unfolding strategy. Some leaders however either don't seem to grasp the importance of this future articulated hope or don't know how to turn it to their advantage. This is strange as the whole point of any change is to shift... to a new place.

Quite reasonably people want to know what this new place looks like before they start. Great leadership knows this and invests time in either:

- constructing and developing a vision with others. I term this as a being a 'developed vision' often constructed through collaboration; or

- selling a vision that is the creative product of an individual or small number of people. 'We just saw what needed to happen' is an indication of a vision that is more 'revelatory' in origin and quality.

Both have their place but the two are different. Leaders get into a muddle when using the language and constructs of revelatory vision to describe what is in essence a developed vision – and of course vice versa... I shall expand on this a little more, later in this section.

Setting sail: Two sources of power to overcome inertia, providing momentum and steerage

The current location is always set against the intended destination and the gap/distance (or in navigational terms, the range) is calculated. The range should never be underestimated or exaggerated. This is the distance that will have to be travelled.

Setting a course to travel between the two places of the 'here and now' and 'there and then' requires power to get there – that is obvious. What is less obvious is just how much power is required to get the ship moving in the first instance.

Leaving port, the ship's engines will be working very hard in the initial stages. Great power precisely delivered is needed to overcome inertia and provide momentum. It is also needed to provide full steerage capability (and therefore control) of the vessel. Again this needs to be applied early on.

In change terms, power comes from the forces pushing you away from the current state and the pull forces of an attracting vision. The dual sources of push and pull power can be boosted and given precision: (a) if intentionality is clear; (b) if the information communicated is robust and believable; and (c) if the leadership work with a sparkling intelligence.

> **// When a 'compelling glimpse of a desired future', provides hope, fosters a strong desire for change with the right mix of the inspirational and the pragmatic, uses technology as the enabler, and sets out values that provide both consistency and glue, then great things can happen.**

The prevailing winds and the tide can buffet ships whose engines are just ticking over in places where manoeuvrability is limited. If the bridge loses command (control), these vessels are termed as 'being adrift'. There are far too many instances where this is happening to organisations in both the private and public sectors. In nautical language this is where the vessel is 'under way but making no way' and it may or may not be 'under command'. This is always a dangerous combination.

Letting go of the old entails risks

Every time I put out to sea I am aware I am taking a risk.

Every experienced seafarer will tell you that the sea, whilst incredibly beautiful, can be hostile and unforgiving. The switch can also happen in the blink of an eye. Therefore it must be for good reason that we let go of the ropes and start moving away from the dockside. The voyage, even on familiar routes, has a habit of throwing up the unexpected and not all disasters happen during raging storms.

The purpose of the voyage really does have to be compelling in order to set sail. Of course we do everything we can to reduce the risk but an element of risk still remains. For any skipper the simplest way of negating much of this is to have (a) a seaworthy vessel that meets or exceeds regulatory requirements; and (b) an experienced and professional crew whom you can trust to do the right thing. You need to know at all times that everyone is doing their job and looking out for each other when things are going well – and when they are going also less well.

The destination has got to be worth the effort and the investment

Getting to where you want to be always has a cost associated with it and this should be understood before embarking on the change. It is also true that very few vessels ever made money staying tied up in harbour, which is why seafarers are also restless folks.

So the intentional destination is of critical importance, as are the values that guide how we all work together to get everyone to that destination. It is for this reason that all of the information from Principle 1 is understood and used to prepare the ship for the voyage. To restate, this information is required and understood in the light of the future shifts required.

This applies equally to those in business and those in the public and social sectors, particularly in the turbulence of today's volatile markets.

It's just a glimpse...

When we talk about our vision, it will always lack some detail because it is about the future and that by definition represents an unknown where not everything is in our control. We can conjecture, we can read trends and interpret patterns, but we don't have a crystal ball. Some might wrongly, but understandably, feel that leaders should indeed have the complete picture in full colour with precise facts and figures at hand ... but the truth is, we never really will.

We do need however to be able to describe the vision with enough clarity and confidence to persuade people that we know reasonably accurately where we are headed and that the pain of leaving the familiar is worth the future opportunity.

Anything less is a betrayal of the people we are asking to come with us on the journey of change.

The vision isn't clear – so do I trust you?

Many leaders lament that their people are slower to adopt the vision than they would like. This is totally understandable because they have not had the same time as the leaders to chew it over and start figuring out the implications beyond how it might affect them. In the initial period the question for those following, who may not understand or embrace the vision in the early stages, is simply: 'Do I trust my leaders?'

If they do trust the leadership, and they see the vision starting to turn from words to something more concrete, they will begin to adopt the future direction for themselves. At this point people will begin to own the vision and great progress can be made.

If they don't trust the leadership there will be continual skirmishes. Those being 'done to' (in their eyes) will try and establish rumours and a counter-narrative. In these cases it is critical to address the issue of lack of trust and deal professionally with the specific points being thrown up. In many instances work that is designed to bolster the vision ends up trying to bring people together in more robust relationships.

If that trust is willfully betrayed, people will never follow the leader again. They may still be managed by them but they will not be followers.

Vision and values

Vision and values are conjoined. Jim Collins and Jerry Porras in a (1996) Harvard Business Review article make a strong play for why the two elements should represent the two streams making up strategic intent. Values outworked through what people actually do and say provide continuity and hold the change together.

Openness and trust are central to all sets of organisational values. Whilst the destination may lack detail, the values that are tangibly outworked provide a confidence in the way the change will be delivered. This is why early on the organisation looks at its leadership and asks 'do I trust them to take me on this journey?'

Navigational Principle 1 creates a push force away from the current reality whist vision exerts a pull towards the desired future. Both are needed to get through the initial stages of the journey, which is often high in expectation and low on certainty. This is referred to as the 'lag phase'. This is why leaders need to be both accurate and truthful around current reality and the intended destination. It is also why the values of honesty and openness are so important.

Vision is neither a speech nor the preserve of visionary types

Many seminars put on to explore the subject of 'vision' use the great speeches of such visionaries as Dr Martin Luther King, Winston Churchill, Mahatma Ghandi, Nelson Mandela, Walt Disney and the like, to show how visions have the capacity to change nations and the very fabric of the way we do things. I love those speeches and take great lessons from them. However, there is a danger. These people are exemplars of and seemingly blessed with, an incredible art and skill that gets used at really important tipping points in history – they are simply outstanding rhetoricians and know how to connect deeply with their intended audiences.

Most of us mere mortals won't reach these dizzy heights of oratory. More to the point, we don't need to. Vision needs to be expressed in our own words and be authentic. Put another way, we need to be the authors of our particular vision.

David, a farmer friend, and I were leaning on a gate looking over one of his fields. We weren't talking much, just enjoying the view, and then he said: 'in this field… you are looking at the future of this farm'. Now to be honest it looked to me just like any other field but what I wasn't seeing was the shift away from using chemicals to control weeds to using more biological methods. This was a big deal and it took some courage from Dave to go organic. It did pay off but he didn't know that at the time… he just had a conviction that this was the right place to aim for. His vision statement was also full of a farmer's gift of understatement!

Some shun the subject of vision altogether and just refer to the 'V-word'; and some just speak of 'direction of travel'. I suspect that this is in part a response to an over-hyping of the concept in previous decades. For a time the concept of vision was positioned in the realms of the mystical and dream worlds. I remember the narrative of the nineties, which was all about the power to 'imagine the impossible'. It can be… but it doesn't have to be.

For a time leaders seemed to be expected to come up with the answers to 'life, the universe and everything' (in The Hitch-hiker's Guide to the Galaxy, Douglas Adams gave the answer as 42) and be able to express this through captivating oratory or some other clever device.

Many leaders just couldn't imagine themselves saying these things so retreated to descriptions of service plans and financial goals. I remember one sales director who did try to explain the future in rather exuberant language with strong 'Churchillian' overtones – and was then asked by one of his team what he had been smoking before the meeting! This wonderfully pithy comment brought the conversation back from outer space and down to earth. Paradoxically a great and inspiring conversation then started and continued over the following months. It was this honest conversation that saw significant improvements in performance. All credit to George the sales director who was big enough and humble enough to be able to laugh at himself.

From my own experience of working in different organisations and in different regions of the world, I would estimate that up to 60% of businesses and other enterprises have currently dispensed with or have seriously diluted the meaning of vision.

So lets reclaim what it actually is.

Reclaiming vision
As has already been stated, vision is a compelling glimpse of a desired future state. It has to resonate with people (which includes the weary and the sceptics), giving hope and purpose now – and not just when the goal is reached sometime in the future.

So it has to be attractive to enough people and make sufficient sense that they can own it for themselves. And stakeholders have to know the leadership believes in it.

At a very simple level vision says 'this is where we are going to'; 'It looks like this'; 'it will enable us to'; 'this is the hope that it represents'; 'this is why we as leaders are investing in this and this will be the opportunity for all of us'…

Those hearing about the vision will need (a) sufficient clarity to begin to form their own picture and start owning it; (b) abundant confidence in the leadership that they have the resources and capability to deliver; (c) an established conviction that this is indeed the way to go; (d) enough certainty that the vision is achievable, with stretch perhaps.

In navigational language vision is spoken of simply as the 'intended destination'. In nautical terms 'intention' denotes that I will do whatever it takes to get there. I will not however expose my vessel or crew and passengers to any more risk than is already inherent in what we are doing.

Because most who earn a living at sea are pragmatists and not poets, our intended destination is pretty much always expressed in quite straightforward terms without too much hype. 'Our berth at Southampton is Port side number 2 and has a great connection to onward travel services…' (This is a bit perfunctory I do admit….!) Some organisations could well do to mix the aspirational and inspirational with the pragmatic. Not everything has to have a strong 'Churchillian' accent.

That said, both elements are important.

An example of this is demonstrated in the museum at Ironbridge celebrating, and illuminating, the industrial revolution. Its value driven goals combined with practical application changed this nation. The combination of the lofty and the pragmatic is still thrilling today, which is why the 'pledge seat' literally a seat in the grounds is covered with promises that inspired visitors make about their future. This is an incredibly moving place to stand and read the comments, while glimpsing the stories that must lie behind the promises 'to self'.

B&Q, the home Improvement business, published their vision some years ago with a mix of honesty and aspiration. Their 'rich picture' literally a picture approximately 3 metres square was a great mix of un-retouched reality, the results of a deep understanding of customers and their market, plus the inspirational and stretch goals so vital to its future. This was all expressed in B&Q language. It remains one of the best expressions of a corporate vision that I have come across in 40 years in business. It has been effective too as it had an adoption rate of over 80% of staff, who knew with real clarity where their job fitted in and who supported the overall change. It has also guided them through the years and helped navigate some pretty challenging markets and competitive trading conditions.

> **Articulating what the future might look like has to resonate with people (which includes the weary and the sceptics), giving hope and purpose now – and not just when the goal is reached sometime in the future.**

It has also to be said that any vision has a limited lifespan because 'shifts, happen'. The hope is that the 3x3m artwork has long been replaced by another compelling picture. With the recent announcement of 'like for like' sales figures down an average of 5%, with outdoor sales of barbeques, external lighting and patio tables and chairs down by over 10%, I hope a new future is already being imagined. This needs to take into account the unpredictable British summer as well as future post-Brexit trading relationships across the globe.

Looking ahead

Almost as a statement of the obvious... the word vision is all about what we 'see'. Seeing is what we do on a continual basis as we look this way and that. What we notice however is rather different.

The first time the captain I worked for gave me the helm, we both looked across the same seascape. What he saw and noticed was a world away from what I was

seeing and noticing. That skill took years to develop as I trained my vision and started to read the shifting picture through the eyes of experience.

What I also did not appreciate at that moment, with my mentor standing next to me, was that he was also seeing a time in the future when he would have a fleet of ferries skippered by those that he had developed, trained and trusted. I became aware of his future vision for the company over the months and years that followed. It all became particularly real when he showed me pictures of vessels that he considered to be beautifully designed and was either going to buy or build. We then started going to shipyards and he took me through the construction process. I then began to really understand in greater depth what he was seeing.

Because future vision is in our mind's eye it is obviously subject to all kinds of challenges and interpretations. However what it does boil down to is a picture clear enough to be grasped, which is loaded with potential. It should communicate the idea 'this is worth going for and investing in'. Sometimes this takes time to come into focus but when people do get it – and particularly other leaders – you can see it in their eyes.

I have seen too many leaders whose eyes are dull and distant as they parrot some strapline about their organisation. You just know they don't feel it, understand it or believe in it. It's just a bunch of words that appear to make sense but don't convey much that is meaningful.

The CEO of a large local council asked us to support the roll-out of his vision. He explained that this repositioning was of real importance to the town he loved, which needed to reclaim its industrial heritage. He said he had been born there, his only passion was for this place and this was to be his last job.

But his eyes said something very different.

I challenged him, to the effect that if we were going to do the work I needed to know the leadership – and him particularly – were committed to the direction being set and that he would be around long enough to see it through. He went quiet and was obviously irritated that I had questioned his commitment. But the truth was that at that time he was in the process of becoming the new CEO of a bigger local authority in another part of the country.

On the other hand when you hear the words of someone who has seen something which resonates, feels achievable, 'if only'... and inspires – literally breathing life into our head and hearts – then you know that they have heard and seen something that has the ability to change situations and people.

If any of us were asked what we see looking ahead to our future of course we wouldn't be able to answer this exactly. Who knows what life has in store? We can however talk about our hopes, dreams and aspirations and what we think could realistically happen. This should be true of all organisations.

Big dreams are all relative

Some individuals seem to dream – 'big dreams'–daring to believe that anything is possible. These represent proponents of the 'Big Hairy Audacious Goals' (BHAGs) that are described by Collins and Porras (1996). Such visions have often created both great successes – and failures and bankruptcies as well. Virgin boss Richard Branson was told at an early age that he would either be arrested or end up a millionaire. He said he did well in achieving both! We need a few of these women and men to challenge convention and mix things up a bit. However we should not see this as the blueprint for how all futures are to imagined.

Daring to believe in a richer future is not just about size or money.

Whilst I was working in a township in Zimbabwe the owner of the very basic home I was being shown around talked about his dream of extending his living area so that he could fit more of his church community in for meals. For him this was one of his life goals and was about serving his community. It was humbling to listen to his story and hear about his big dream.

A woman in the Ukraine who was a participant on a business course I was delivering talked about opening a beauty salon. This had been her lifelong ambition but she thought it would never come to anything under the old Soviet regime. Now she was free to live her dream – and her delight was mingled with her tears, as she shared how she was about to open her first salon.

When Darwin E. Smith became the CEO of Kimberly Clarke, many regarded him as underqualified for the position. They failed to recognise the emergence of one of the most successful businessmen of his time. He saw that continuing to run expensive paper mills producing coated paper was going to limit the company to a future of mediocrity. His solution was to close the mills and concentrate on paper-based products like disposable nappies and then the company moved into hand dryers. 'The rest is history', as they say.

And trending…. Following years of research, some farms are being encouraged to adopt a 'no plough regime'. Convention from earliest times would see the soil broken up by a plough and prepared for seeding. Now it seems that this damages soil structure, reduces drainage and increases erosion and nitrogen run-off. 'The no plough system' relies on applying organic matter

and establishing large worm populations that convert the plant material into fertiliser and provide good drainage holes. In trials, yields are up and erosion and nitrogen run-off are down… another vision for a richer more sustainable future. This will be a big deal for some farms and environmentalists as well.

Importance of calibrating language

So 'big' is a relative term but at the heart of it, it is an attempt, I think, to convey that the future has potential, promise and hope.

It is to everyone's advantage if the size of the vision is discussed, calibrated and agreed so that terminology doesn't say one thing and mean another. This agreement also begins to define the effort needed to realise the vision.

The process and size of any change can also be described in different ways: (a) transformational; (b) transitional; and (c) developmental. There seems to be a current trend to call everything transformational, whilst ignoring the developmental and the transitional. It is important to calibrate the size of the change and express this accurately so as to avoid confusion and undirected effort. Simple developmental shifts often yield significant cost savings – so why confuse language and call it transformational when it does not need to be this form?

Daring to believe in a richer future is not just about size or money.

At the core, hope

Looking ahead has to focus on hope and as I have already mentioned the scale of the change is relative to context and situation. Vision is fundamentally an attracting force pulling you forward towards a future place. In this case, hope pulls you through – this is the second part of the Stockdale principle (Collins, 2001).

The ancient Wisdom texts in the Hebrew Bible say that without a vision (hope) we shrivel and die (Proverbs 29.18). My observation is that sometimes people (and organisations) just shrivel.

Vision sometimes needs resetting

I have seen a recent example of where vision needed to be reset on the lines of Isaiah Berlin's 'hedgehog' principle (Collins, 2001).

A landscaping and water garden business that was once very successful had fallen on harder times for a whole variety of factors. This included having no strategy to deal with competing sales of cheap equipment on the internet. Recently it has had to sell off much of its grounds and showroom in order to survive.

Now it operates with just a quarter of the original land and has a converted shipping container as an office. This is different from the extensive showroom of just one year ago. However its core business of landscaping large estates and municipal gardens remains very much intact and the future feels more realistic and positive. Despite this, the mood of the team is sullen and dispirited. I do understand this, as just glancing around at the visible assets it has the feel of a business that is wasting away, particularly for the management team who have spent years always thinking bigger.

However the reality is that everything seems to be in place for what could be a productive and profitable future. What has to change are the attitudes and behaviour of the owners and their team and this is no small challenge. They see scaling back as failure, and this sense is passed on to their customers. What they have yet to discover is that by getting back to their core products and services, this reduction could have saved the business and given them a future. I hope that this turns out to be the case but the restructuring now needed is in their heads.

In this case, hope is not about bigger, better and more diverse. It's about going back to what the company excels at, what the money will allow them to do and what is the real passion of those founding the business. This had been about massive landscaping projects creating stunning lakes and ponds. Indeed, the showroom may well have been a project of hubris.

Hope potentially exists and in the leaner picture of the operation there exists a different vision. It is there if they choose to see it in a business that has had to return to what it does best but without all of the periphery activity and cost that wasn't producing revenue.

This is a reminder to all that vision does not automatically mean growth and expansion and may sometimes need to be reset according to the resources we have to invest. I hope my friends will come to realise that in a tighter run and more focused business, there is hope.

Vision so far...
Up to this point we have looked at these aspects of vision:

- Vision should address the question of 'where we are going', making clear the values and beliefs that underpin the journey. This is why 'vision and values' are spoken of together.

- Vision is also about seeing what is going on around you in real time.

- In organisational terms 'vision and values' should resonate with the hopes of the wider community.

- Sometimes this amplifies what others are already seeing and describing and at other times it is giving it a voice to the unexpressed.

- Sometimes, of course, it takes a while for people to get on board, particularly with future direction, but when individuals and teams start owning the future for themselves all kinds of things become possible.

- Vision should be compelling before the change starts and draw people towards this future place. Some make the mistake of implying that once we have gone through the pain everyone will then understand why it's all been worth it. This equates to 'jam tomorrow' and is largely ineffective.

- In their description of a multifaceted vision, Collins and Porrit (1996) pictorially describe two strands, which equate to 'direction' and then 'beliefs and values'. Again there is a mix of the inspirational and the pragmatic.

If it were that simple...
I hope what is coming across is that vision has many facets and nuances and getting it right requires an investment of time and energy either in its formation or articulation.

Under pressure leaders and managers sometimes try to skip the full investment required and what gets constructed and talked about creates confusion rather than clarity. This in turn amplifies cynicism rather than confidence and hope. This is why some leaders have dropped the term, vision, in favour of the term 'direction of travel' as it might appear to be a less arduous thing to describe. For reasons already given I think this dilutes meaning too much but I do understand that some leaders work in such toxic situations that any vision statement might be career limiting. This is why courage always plays its part in any successful change.

I would recommend that in such political situations a better term would be 'our course towards'. In navigational terms this preserves some degree of intentional direction.

Straplines are not visions
I am surprised how many organisations and leaders use the 'strapline' to wholly replace or articulate vision. Straplines are very useful when the depth of meaning is understood and people recognise and associate with it. At times it is important to gather around a theme. They can also be a lazy way of trying to convey future direction. Many straplines have a porosity of real meaning and are little more than slogans.

We should all remember the disastrous Conservative slogan of the 2017 'snap' general election, repeated at every opportunity. It most certainly did not produce 'strong and stable government'. Misused slogans cause people to respond with increasing derision and cynicism. What we all want is to know is 'so what do you see honestly for the future?'

And to make things even more complex...

'Tomorrow's Council today' was initially a meaningless slogan to the majority of employees and residents of a local authority. It was also a meaningless term to half of the senior management team that were supposed to be delivering it and providing an example of what it meant. For most, 'the vision' lacked pretty much everything of any importance. It certainly didn't pass the test of any robust vision where the criteria asks whether there is (a) clarity of direction; (b) conviction that this is the right way to go; (c) certainty that the right resources to complete the journey are available; (d) confidence in the leadership.

Working with the senior team and starting with their strapline of 'Tomorrow's Council today' it was very clear that half of the group were also very possessive of what they referred to as 'their vision'. The other half had no clue what it meant. Trying to get beyond what was a rather blocked situation, we kept asking 'so what does that mean?' This was in an attempt to go beyond the words. The owners of the strapline just could not see how, to half of the executive, it was just meaningless drivel.

Slowly what emerged was a story of how some of the older team had had a very powerful and productive workshop a couple of years ago where the group worked with skill and depth to figure out what the future might look like. They rolled up all of the arguments, debates and the time of consensus into just three words. And to them this strapline conjured up all of the conversations and decisions that took place in what was a significant two-day event.

The issue was that half of the team of senior leaders weren't at the workshop and neither were the rest of their organisations. Put simply the CEO and those present two years before had communicated the strapline but not the deeper meaning and the newer members of the executive hadn't pressed for clarification.

We revisited the themes and the debates and at this point the whole executive began to get the picture. We then asked them to describe this pictorially and in a language others would understand, and a rich picture began to emerge. This then informed a comprehensive and intelligent strategy, which steered their authority through some pretty rough seas as austerity funding took hold. They became one of the more successful authorities in the UK.

Vision is not a document

Over a six-year period and then every two years I was asked by a large aid organisation to help them review their vision and strategy. Before our conversations started, they would send me a bound 200-page plus version of their current vision. Every time I studied it (I must admit, losing the will to live at times) I discovered that just a couple of other leaders had taken time to also read it. Even the multiple authors of various sections hadn't bothered to read the entire document.

The detail was both a reflection of their culture, which seemed to come alive in the minutiae of plans and the highly regulated world they worked in. Despite this, the document gave little clarity about the future intended course. It did have 'thud' value as its great weight landed on people's desks but it wasn't compelling in any way. Some good work had gone into its preparation but this wasn't about vision. In the end we got them to forgo, with great reluctance, the pretence of reviewing the expanding document and work on creating a shared understanding between stakeholders of what they really wanted to achieve. They got there in the end but still produce documents of 50-pages plus... but that is progress!

And neither does it live in a briefcase

We were invited by the executive of a large government department to help them translate a vision into practical outcomes. This sounded quite an interesting piece of work. However confusion took hold when we asked, at the start of a two-day team meeting, what the vision was and could they put the description, picture and/or model of it up in front of us. This was so that we could continually come back and check all the work fitted with their overall intent.

They responded by saying that they had indeed done the work to imagine the future and that 'Mike' had picked up the vision, after the last workshop. Mike searched his briefcase but didn't come up with it. No, they said. Karen must have picked it up. Karen looked unconvinced and began with increasing desperation going through her bags. Now everyone was looking for whatever this thing was. After ten minutes the CEO looked up and said, 'Sorry we must have left the vision back in the office!' If you knew which department this was you might not be too surprised! You just can't make this stuff up!

Vision has to have life, be describable and be owned at the start of a change particularly amongst the leaders who have developed it. If leaders don't have it residing in their heads and hearts and if they really don't believe in it, then it really won't happen. I promise you – it won't happen. It didn't in the case of this government department.

Seeing... when you are part of the culture

Trying to 'see' in a culture which you are part of is also fraught with challenges.

Can't see... Won't see... Won't change

A very British and hierarchical business knew that it needed to reform. As part of the vision it had imagined an empowered, less stuffy and more open culture. Its vision was expressed as 'creating a place of open doors' for customers and employees alike. All seemed genuinely excited about the change. What was amusing however was that when we went to see the CEO we walked down a corridor, which was some 50 metres long, and every solid big oak door was very firmly shut. On each door was the occupant's last name and their title. It said so much of the existing culture.

Knocking on the closed door of the PA to the CEO, my colleague and I had to work very hard to refrain from fits of laughter as we as we stared into the face of this rather obvious contradiction. By the time we were talking to some of the senior leaders about their 'open door vision' we were really struggling to keep things together. We took everyone outside to look at the corridor of closed oak doors behind which 'who knows what' was going on. We asked what plans they had to refurbish the offices and they looked horrified that we had even asked. There were no plans... With some frustration on their part they got us back into the room to talk about the open door vision. They just couldn't see what to everyone who visited the building was so obvious. If you are in the system it is sometimes very difficult to see with a degree of objectivity. And of course, for this organisation, despite a great sounding change programme.... nothing changed.

Can't see... Now can see... Will change

Working with the executive of a large organisation, everyone had become blocked in one session that was considering how to implement an empowering culture. We took a break. The men's and women's toilets were next to each other and when my colleague and I had finished our comfort visit (as they call it in the US), we arrived in the corridor together. I asked how many she had spotted in the woman's toilets. '13' she replied. In the men's there were 11. We both knew what the other had seen and at that point we knew what the issue was. We got the executives to reassemble in the loos against the obvious background of ribaldry and bewilderment and asked what did they see? After all the predictable comments they began to notice all the signs and messages were framed as a negative injunction or just felt aggressive. 'Don't leave taps running', 'Wash your hands', 'Don't throw paper towels down the toilet', 'No paper towels in this bin'... and so on.

'Wow' they said. 'Never seen this before... it's a bit negative isn't it?' In response we said we had a theory, so we took the lift down to the ground floor and reception. There was no welcome for staff and visitors only more signs set in negative language. We walked them through the building and more of the same become so obvious. The whole feeling of the building was summarised by

them as being like... 'The answer is NO... so what's your question?'...!

The signage was both an expression of a previous culture that they were moving away from and was also creating a heaviness that was greater than just the messages.

So the intervention was to remove all of the negative stuff and replace with a welcome in reception and positive notices throughout. In six months the atmosphere was so different. It was then they asked ... 'So how come we hadn't seen this before?' We responded that if you are in it, it becomes very difficult to see through independent eyes.

The above example is inevitable. We will always be part of the system that employs us, taking on, to a greater or lesser extent, the patterns and behaviour that exists. This is where an outside view is very helpful as it has the potential to see what others cannot.

> So the intervention was to remove all of the negative stuff and replace with a welcome in reception and positive notices throughout. In six months the atmosphere was so different.

Vision is not permanent – there is always another horizon

Thirty-five years ago I sat around a wood fire, chatting with a friend who was an officer in the British army. We had cooked a great meal made from wild ingredients and were enjoying a couple of cans of beer or 'frosties' as the Africans call them. We started to talk about the future and how we could make a living doing the things we loved. As we talked it was as if we could see the years ahead with some colour and exciting detail. It felt compelling enough for us to consider leaving our secure jobs. At that moment a seed was planted in both of us.

Years have gone by and we have both realised much of what we saw around that fire. However it has turned out to be in very different ways than expected. Frans, who grew up in the African bush, was a survival expert and a tracker. He eventually went on to work with a children's charity in the war-torn regions of Africa. His job was to go deep into conflict areas and to set up secure transition bases for getting women and children out and into safe camps. When captured a few years ago by Somali rebels all thought he would be murdered. But such was his relationship with the local tribes that they stepped in on his behalf and miraculously secured his release (Daily Mail, 2010).

My journey was very different. I worked for an American computer corporation, travelled the world and pioneered with colleagues from other companies some of the stuff my younger colleagues now tell me they invented. I moved on and with a few friends founded Teleios Consulting twenty years ago.

Both Frans and I stayed true to the fundamentals of what we had glimpsed years before around that fire but we have flexed and changed direction where we needed to or where one set of goals had been achieved. Our course has stayed true and our journeys have taken us on many different paths. We found that there was always a different horizon when we approached what was the original objective.

In my career too I had the privilege of working for the Digital Equipment Company, known as DEC by customers and the market. Its founder Ken Olsen, a global award-winning entrepreneur and all round good guy, was captivated by technology. He built his first 'super computer' in his garage just outside of Boston. It became the industry leader and the company grew to an enormous size, second only to IBM.

Ken's vision, which had seen the rise of the 'mainframe' and incredible computer capability, had however, never moved on. So when he was asked about the future and would DEC adopt desktop technology, he is reported to have said…"who would want a computer sat on their desk?' (!) And that was the beginning of the end.

Vision is not a permanent fixed position but shifts and changes, offering either adventure or obsolescence.

Two potential origins, two different strategies

Vision can be revelatory, in that it becomes revealed and obvious in just a moment of time. The conversation around the fire with my friend Frans is an example of this. Often inspiration arrives in the strangest moments, taking the person(s) by surprise. This can result in hurriedly scribbled down notes, diagrams or mind maps on any scrap of paper as a way of recording the moment. Revelatory vision is compelling for those who have seen it, but then requires a 'sell' to bring on board the majority who weren't at the workshop, chatting over coffee or scribbling on a scrap of paper….

The alternative is that it is developed with many contributions, working and moulding and testing what people have seen. The result is the product of much hard work that has been developed over time. Developed vision by definition has involved normally a greater

sphere of contributors, so has less issues trying to persuade people… but it is slow and messy.

The fact that revelatory and developed vision are derived from two different constructs is a point that is missed frequently. Both types of vision are legitimate and have a place in business, but each requires a different set of explanations, along with different selling and engagement strategies, to get the vision into the heads and hearts of those who are following.

A misunderstanding also occurs because of how the term, vision, has been overused and mythologised over the past few decades. In reality a lot of the teaching and training on the subject has used the revelatory constructs associated with stories like St Paul on the road to Damascus or the great speeches of Martin Luther King, Churchill, Ghandi, Mandela and the like. In contrast much vision in business has been the result of hard work and experience developed over time and is by nature more fluid and organic. The 'no plough regime' mentioned earlier is a good example of a 'developed vision'.

To restate, both have a place but require different approaches and narratives to help people make sense of them.

> Vision is not a permanent fixed position but shifts and changes, offering either adventure or obsolescence.

Tapping into a hope that already exists

When Martin Luther King declared: 'I have a dream….', to this day the picture of the future he described is spine-tingling as it resonates with a deeper hope that good people share. One day many still hope to see it become our living reality. It still catches people's deep desires.

This in part is because what he described was a hope that already resided in people's hearts and minds. He gave expression to it in a way that caused people to say: 'That's it… that's what I feel… I am recognising it in the words that I hear.' So it resonated with a deep and previously held conviction, which formerly lacked the words of expression. These are still incredible moments in history.

In business we may not always be dealing with such lofty themes but the principle of finding visions that resonate with existing hope is still very important.

For those who have dedicated their lives to making a difference in communities, or those whose passion is to get 'through life housing' adopted by planners and construction companies…. When others speak of vision they are listening to hear how… this technology, or that reorganisation… will help in the delivery of their work. Repetitive Process Automation (RPA) probably won't get most of our pulses racing with inspiration (although it will for some with a more technical bias), however if it frees up resource to help the homeless then social workers, the police, and the ambulance service could get a little excited!

All vision, regardless of origin, requires the four Cs of clarity, conviction, confidence and commitment that we have mentioned before, and if conveyed authentically can still tap into the unexpressed hope of people. If enough people begin to see it then the slight pull becomes a strong draw towards this described future.

When I asked B&Q if their 'rich picture' was more than just some images and words framed cleverly, they told me that the independent research said that 80% of the workforce understood the picture. Simply put, 'they got it'. In 'getting it' they could:

- describe it;

- understand it;

- feel it was the right way to go;

- be motivated by it; and

- know where their jobs fitted into it.

That is a high percentage and demonstrates how a developed vision democratises the effort and can create momentum. The confidence of the workforce increased as they saw how the practical outworking of the vision made a positive impact on the business. Saying you believe in eco-positive products is given real meaning if you pull from the shop floor patio heaters that aren't so eco-friendly. B&Q did this, at their substantial cost, but in turn won the loyalty of customers and employees alike. Great values and astute business acumen applied.

A fear of expressing vision

As has already been noted throughout this book an increasing number of CEOs don't like the term, vision, and intentionally replace it with, direction of travel, instead. Given the toxicity of their context I do understand their reluctance, although I still feel it sells their organisations short.

One CEO who had been accused of a lack of vision by some politicians and some of his own staff said, when challenged, 'I saw what the politicians did to my predecessors who dared to publish their vision… they were used as political footballs at the cost to our service. I will not make the same mistake.' I have great respect for this leader. I have seen them navigate with real skill scrutiny committees, avoiding the traps being set by one or two of the more duplicitous members for their own ambitions and agenda. Fortunately the majority of the cross-party membership seemed more intelligent and switched on. I have seen them, too, champion minorities, creating a fairer playing field of job opportunity and the promotion of the place where they lived and loved.

I do understand why the CEO was reluctant to come out with what he saw, but my observation is that employees were somewhat confused about what the future held. They grasped that this was a time of massive change but were less than convinced that the future had any degree of intentional clarity or purposeful direction.

In this case I know that the CEO did have vision but it was unexpressed.

Some colleagues had picked up on a growing feeling that the vision wasn't clear and were raising concerns. The team of consultants I was working with invited the CEO to a session without agenda to talk through what they were seeing for the organisation and the city where they were based. The leader addressed some of the senior colleagues who privately were beginning to think that the CEO was adrift.

Two hours later, having told a few very funny and poignant anecdotes, disclosed some very personal stuff, passionately talked about place and people and the organisation that they loved, there was initially silence. In that relatively short time they had indeed all glimpsed a compelling future… This was the second bit of the change picture – they all knew why the current situation was unsustainable, but they didn't know previously where they were going.

Now they saw.

For me the sad thing in this situation was that those revealing two hours should have been the springboard for a service-wide communication resulting in many others 'seeing' as well. However it stayed within this small group and even the CEO's most senior colleagues who weren't at the meeting kept asking 'so what is the vision?' It was there in inspiring detail but it t was largely unexpressed and remained a mystery to the majority.

Fear, however legitimate, had stopped the good news getting out and the feeling of drift was too prevalent. This was a case where the 'direction of travel' explanations gave away little of the real vision…. which did exist. I think this was an opportunity missed.

It's right to weigh the cost

So visions will cost and it is right to weigh this up. Ultimately the leader has to make a judgement call about whether they are prepared to pay or not. Navigation after all is about making choices. Visions can be contentious but they are still critical to answering the simple question from employees which is: 'So what does this future look like?'

As already and frequently mentioned, one of the most comprehensive and positive visions I have come across is the one that underpinned the major change in the DIY store B&Q. Some twelve years ago they were fighting for their survival in a very competitive and overcrowded market. Several of their competitors had gone under.

As good navigators they took time out to consider the three questions of navigation.

- Where are we... really?

- Where do we want to get to?

- How are we going to get there?

The detailed answers were put into B&Q language and represented as a journey at sea on a very large canvas.

1 Where are we now...? Their location was described as being under storm clouds with high-cost sandbanks all around them. Their description of their current reality was uncompromising.

2 A postcard from the future. Where they wanted to get to had broad appeal and depth and included a desire to transform the customer experience. The hiring of former trades people to give informed advice was elegant and simple.

3 What we know of our journey. They knew they had to avoid the high-cost sand banks that could run them aground. This formed the basis of the buyers' negotiating strategy with suppliers over price and terms and conditions. To increase footfall they needed to differentiate between sets of customer requirements, giving each what was specifically being asked for. This was practically outworked in the products range, pricing and support services. And all of this was outworked through the B&Q value set.

The picture, rich in both detail and meaning, was displayed in staff areas – it was colourful, engaging, informative and clear. Behind the picture was a vast database of information that was available to all – it wasn't just about pretty pictures but about detail and how decisions were taken. This was the basis of the B&Q reinvention.

Having been successful in both surviving and making the enterprise more customer aware, the challenge now is to keep doing this and keep reinventing.
There is no such thing as sustained strategic advantage as a one-off event – it has to be continually pursued.

What do we see our technology delivering?

When I was a captain I thought we had some important and what seemed 'smart' technology to help navigate and inform choices and decisions. These days, in order to keep contact with the sea, I have a boat which is packed full of electronics, computers and incredible software. Even on my small cruiser the technology is so far away from what we had 40 years ago. However for fun I still use my old gear from time to time. This is why I am amused and comforted that the US navy is going to start again training all of its officers and cadets in using the compass, sextant and pencils. This is obviously about building resilience in case of cyber attack but I hope also it is about helping all to understand how navigational thinking and principles have to be foundational to emerging technology. Knowing this will only enhance our use of technology allowing it to deliver the promised transformative futures.

Bear in mind, though, that Klaus Schwab of the WEF reminds us all that digital technology consists of 'tools made by people for the benefit of people' (World Economic Forum, 2016). I along with many others hope that the 'people' in this description is our human race and not just a few very powerful individuals and corporations. I guess that this too is subject to the choices the WEF are referring to in their paper.

Twenty years ago we talked about the digital revolution. Little did many of us, even from within the industry, think that today we would still be looking at digital horizons and be talking about the transformation yet to come. Many glimpse its importance, but few have grasped the real implications. Most businesses and the public sector are in catch-up mode.

For leaders there will be many questions to wrestle with and find answers to. One obvious one that strikes me is how leadership and navigation, which rely on choices and decision taking, will interface with artificial intelligence (AI) and the system's autonomous decision making processes? Given that navigation is all about making choices this could prove to be an interesting and challenging area to figure out. I would go as far as to say that who (or what) makes choices will become the contested subject of the future.

Leaders who 'live' visions bring about change

When Jim Collins published Good to Great (2001) there were some interesting data and patterns tucked away in the research that were noted, but didn't have prominence. This fascinated me. One example is that the vast majority of leaders who could be described as being at Level 7 had gone through their own personal transformation as a result of some major life event.

I have observed over the years that some men and women who have gone through life's crucible seem to 'see' in a different way. Their perspective gets enriched, gets broader and deeper – in short it gets transformed. This in turn affects the way they lead their organisations and their presence conveys an authority that is not about title or position.

As a person who has been involved in developing leaders over the years the above presents some interesting responses. Clearly these dramatic times can't be engineered, although I have seen a temptation presented by Jim's study for a few, not-so-bright leaders to try to book on the 'being humble' workshop….

However I have more importantly recognised common patterns emerge in those who have gone through life's fire in the way they respond to the experience. Central to this is the way they have chosen to react. They choose not to get bitter, they choose not to close down and withdraw, they choose to learn and keep hoping and they choose to forgive rather than be prisoners. They 'rub out, not rub in' as my friend Dave Hill, CEO of HeartSmart, describes it. If the crucible and the heat results in fluidity and the disruption of past patterns, then it is choice that determines what comes next….

As we can't engineer such life-changing events, perhaps a different way for leaders to develop comes back to simply being open and fluid enough in the day to day moments of life. Becoming a grandparent has been a delight for me, and I absolutely love to spend time with Caleb and Maddie, watching them grow and develop. They have given both joy and a sense of time passing, reigniting a desire I have to make a difference in whatever time I have left on this earth. My family tell me I am different in a good way having spent time with them both. My time in Africa has also challenged my views in some surprising ways. I am still trying to make sense of the contradictions and emotions, seeing real hopelessness on the ground in the midst of which there is always resilience, dignity and faith that things could get better. Getting older too is having impact in so many ways, as Stevie Nicks poetically explored in the (1973) song 'Landslides'.

So I have had no crucibles as such… but simply life's ongoing challenge to learn and grow.

Summary
Vision by its very nature is about imagery, pictures and what we see. It should be able to generate in our mind's eye a clear representation of the future that resonates. Without direction and hope organisations shrivel and die. Vision is a essential part of the three navigational questions.

Diluting the role played by vision in creating movement in change programmes will reduce the forces available to overcome inertia. In other words, not much will shift. Vision is either revelatory or developed both are legitimate for change but require different languages and constructs to be effective.

Vision has a clear and intended direction. It also outlines the value set that will govern behaviour and particularly decision making and taking.

Vision has to pass the test of clarity, conviction, certainty and confidence. It has to be expressed in a language understood by the organisation. It has to be compelling enough now to make the change not just make sense when the destination has been achieved.

The destination lies in the future, so it is always expressed as the intended destination because we are not in control of everything nor indeed do we know everything.

> Vision has a clear and intended direction. It also outlines the value set that will govern behaviour and particularly decision making and taking.

Visions have a cost line – they are never free.

Visions should produce enthusiasm and engagement.

Effective leadership and vision should be intertwined.

Leaders should live the change they want to see in others.

There is always a new horizon replacing the old – visions change.

Visions have to be scrutinised by a repetition of the simple question 'so what do we mean by…?'

Vision has to be expressed in multiple ways for people to begin to understand it.

Vision should be translated into mission, strategy, and operational goals in a way that allows everyone to trace their job descriptions back into the organisational vision.

Digital Transformation is still misunderstood and therefore offers major traps and incredible opportunities

Some questions

- What is your intended destination?

- How clear is that destination to you and your team? How do you know?

- Does this destination produce engaged conversations and enthusiasm?

- As a visitor to your organisation could I see the intended destination and make sense of it?

- Can you describe the vision of your business without referring to any notes? In other words does the vision reside in you?

- Are you convinced and willing to pay the cost of seeing this vision come into being?

- Are you personally excited about the future and does it to you present hope?

- In your organisation how many would be able to describe and associate with the vision?

- Would it pass the test of clarity, conviction, certainty and confidence for several layers of the organisation below senior management?

- To what extent is the vision pulling people towards your desired future?

- Do you personally believe in the vision?

- How much are you personally willing to invest to see it come about?

- Does the vision adequately express hope?

- Are the organisation's values sufficiently obvious in the behaviour of the senior leaders?

- Are they particularly prominent when everyone is under pressure?

- How are the senior team making sure they are seeing accurately all that is going on in the organisation and in the wider context?

Bringing together the key themes of this section and concluding remarks

If the work looking forward is done well and the vision is clear, believable, compelling and energising then a critically important attracting force will have been established. At the heart of this is hope. Without hope we just go through the motions. And most significantly of all change is about shifting to a better place. It really is that simple.

Combining Navigational Principles 1 & 2

Current position and the future destination will highlight the distance to be travelled. This will have an investment implication. It will also determine the mix of driving and attracting forces being described / experienced and implications.

Knowing where you are in enough detail to answer the 'why' change question, along with the attraction of a future destination, provides two critical forces. Movement starts when the sum of these two forces is greater than the inertia of the status quo.

Before considering the third element of navigation – which is 'how are we going to get there....?' – I want to put this into the context of the first two questions of 'why' and 'where'.

In all change programmes... momentum is everything

In change, momentum is all. It takes a lot of effort to get what Jim Collins (2001) refers to as the 'build up, breakthrough flywheel' moving. This huge investment of effort at the start is critical for future success. Overcoming the inertia of existing patterns of practice and behaviour does require a great deal of effort and this comes from the power generated in the first two questions of navigation. These are identified as push and pull forces.

Moving away from an unsustainable current reality is normally felt as a push force. The vision on the other hand is an attracting force so it will be experienced as a pull towards something. In most situations it will be the combination of the two that will free a business from the status quo and begin to propel it forwards. However as a leader it is wise to know what proportion each of these very different forces is playing out in the organisation. It is important to know as the messaging and narrative will need to take this into account. Therefore, to explain a little...

If the reason for the change is primarily about getting away from an unsustainable current reality (because things could well come crashing down) then the message from leaders needs first to acknowledge the uncertainty and pain being experienced. It is wise to get alongside people and then gently, clearly and with confidence talk about future possibilities. Too often I have seen excitable leaders 'big up' the vision without acknowledging the

many people who are bruised, sceptical, and with eyes still looking back towards how it used to be. They understand the need to change but they hurt as the loss is felt keenly.

If the energy is all about the vision and what the enterprise could become, then it is wise to let this run and appropriately remind people why the organisation could not just continue on in the same way. Sometimes the excitement of future direction needs a little grounding (but not too much or this will shift the mood and momentum will be lost).

All pull and little push...

One local authority we worked alongside was based in an affluent market town within commuting distance of London. It was leafy, prosperous and a great place to be. The council wanted to grow the town a little and there was money to do so.

> **Overcoming the inertia of existing patterns of practice and behaviour does require a great deal of effort and this comes from the power generated in the first two questions of navigation.**

Its vision was to keep everything that was good about the place and to add a business park aimed at innovation and entrepreneurs. It wanted to be a leading player in the production of high tech solutions and not just a dormitory town for London. Every time this was discussed there was much enthusiasm and no real blocks but nothing ever seemed to progress. After a couple of years, despite the fact that everyone thought it was the right way forward the vision effectively shrivelled up and no change happened and no dream was realised. The pull was strong but the push forces were notably absent, certainly in enough strength.

The result was that status quo was maintained.

All push with little pull...

In another organisation, a change in technology, rising production costs and much thinner margins meant that the executives were facing, for the first time in the company's history of stellar growth, the prospect of takeover. Their response was to try to galvanise the business into action simply on the premise that the current position was unsustainable. They cut wherever they could and beyond. They stoked multiple fires and there was frenetic activity. The vision was simply a meaningless strapline. After many false starts and floundering around they were taken over and lost all they had once dreamed of. In one of the world's largest corporate acquisitions, a lack of vision had brought one of our greatest and most innovative companies to an ignoble end.

The forces driving away from an unsustainable current reality were very strong but the absence of any meaningful vision meant that the question about direction was left unanswered. There were many false starts. A number of high profile acquisitions that had not been strategically thought through, didn't deliver ether direction or advantage. The company was felt by many observers to be rudderless and adrift. Even in its newly acquired colours and under new leadership the drift is still very visible.

Moving the breakthrough flywheel

Thus all change programmes need to have both push and pull forces operating, although not necessarily in equal measures. The combination of both has to be sufficient to overcome the cultural and operating inertia. The narrative of the change will also be affected by the ratio of the push and pull forces in operation and this is why the leaders need to understand how that ratio is being perceived and enacted throughout the organisation. To achieve this the leadership needs to be in close contact with their organisation(s) and have direct and open communications. The presence of any filters via programme teams, interim directors and more formal communication processes can distort the message. Leaders do need to know what is being talked about around the coffee machines in the honest tones that make up such conversations.

It helps if the culture is open and in these circumstances it simply requires the right connections to be made throughout the enterprise. If the culture is closed this will amplify the disconnectedness of the organisation and result in poor decision making. This is why Patrick Lencioni (2002) asserts that trust is everything.

At the time of writing I am aware of three major change programmes being delivered by leaderships that are dysfunctional. Already they are hitting issues and I doubt very much whether any significant change will be achieved despite the structural reorganisations. Things will only turn around if the senior relationships are improved, and trust and cooperation is re-established. The question is, are these people willing to make the effort to sort things out? With help each of the three situations can be turned around if the relationships are transformed first.

If they grasp the truth that the dysfunctional relationships will stop organisational transformation and then if they can begin to see that they can be around each other in productive ways without even liking each other ... then progress is possible.

I am confident that even in the most dysfunctional of teams, progress is always possible as long as there is the will to try. We were asked by the CEO of one of the world's leading digital securities company to help them integrate with the corporation who had just bought them out. They were really struggling. In a senior team of 12 people they had 4 or 5 of the world's leading experts. The CEO said that the problem was 'they hated him, they hated each other and we are stuck'. He continued... 'I don't need them to love or even like each other but I do need them to work productively together'. One of my colleagues bravely took the brief and skilfully got them to acknowledge the current state of things and understand the consequences to each of them if the situation was left to continue. He then got them to imagine in very pragmatic ways what working productively with each other, whilst not 'loving' each other, might look like. This was enough to shift a stuck situation and good progress was made. Push and pull in operation!

> They hate me and they hate each other...
> I don't need them to love or even like each other but I do need them to work productively together... CEO of digital securities company.

Navigational Principle 3

So how do we practically and successfully make the shift?

All of the preparation finally boils down to the actual shift or the journey. There is much that can be foreseen if we use our eyes and engage both common sense and intelligence. This will be translated into a dynamic plan where we will model the way ahead. And then, of course, there are all of the 'off plan' events that demand coodinated responses. On ships, the bridge is a place of great activity, watchfulness, of authority and a place of calm, each doing their job.

Waymarks to navigate this section

'How are we going to get to our intended destination?' is, indeed, the crunch question. All leaders are ultimately judged on their response.

The answer will begin to pull in all of the work from the first two navigational principles. It will also signal to all what values will guide the work and how practical decisions will get made and implemented. This will be further interpreted in the light of the key question asked by employees which is: 'So what is going to happen to my job, my team and my service?'

Setting out

On the chart table of all commercial vessels, and most pleasure craft, will be the chart or charts that cover the whole voyage. These extraordinary sources of information are the product of huge investments of time to survey, measure, amend and update the data recorded over centuries of effort. To me they are almost works of art. The history of cartography is a story in itself and is fascinating.

Charts contain information about the underwater seascape, showing banks and channels and outcrops of rock. This is all laid out on a grid so that I can calculate exactly where I am, using lines of longitude and latitude. There will be information about hazards, tidal flows and tidal races. I will be able to avoid, or indeed find, wrecks depending on the purpose of the voyage. The buoys showing channels will be marked, noting their specific and signatory lights so critical for night-time navigation. Distances will be set down using a known and calibrated scale.

If the charts are not up to date or a bit light on specifics, I will have invested time in talking to people who may have relevant experience. This helps me build some sort of picture in my head that gets used in conjunction with real-time observation of the seascape being travelled through.

Added to this will be information from tide tables about tidal speed and the range of the rise and fall. I will have up to date weather charts on my screens with the predictive forecast over the next hours and days. And for good measure I will have an array of computers and other instrumentation including radar, sonar, radio and a host of sensors providing real-time information about the vessel's operating systems.

So whether I am travelling by day or night I will have a lot of information to help me make and take decisions.

In the UK we are blessed with charts that are pretty accurate. In other parts of the world they can be more flimsy but mariners use what they have got to hand. This includes local knowledge from other sea users including pilots and fishermen who have an intimate picture of the local conditions and the seabed and how this influences vessels on the surface.

All of this informs the practical decisions of navigation but relies on the captain and crew putting together multiple streams of information.

So if I were the skipper of a small cruiser coming out of Poole Harbour and setting out towards Weymouth, the chart would tell me where there were tide races and on what state of the tide these would happen. Going past Old Harry Rocks on a flood tide means that the tide race is not a major risk and I could keep close in to shore. On an ebb tide I would not want to do this, particularly if the tide was a 'spring ebb' with a strong south-westerly wind. In this instance I would take a route further out to sea, which would burn more fuel but be safer. In this example I will have used information from chart, tide tables, and weather forecasts, augmented by my first-hand experience of various conditions.

Most critically my decision about heading and speed will also be informed by looking out of the window and over the sea.

So the preparation is extensive and informed. It is also sequenced so I will know what I should be doing and when during the preparation for and initial moments of the voyage. From the moment a ship leaves the safety of its berth on the dockside, it will be travelling towards its intended destination. The route that it takes, if tracked, would show many changes in direction and speed as it makes multiple and continual choices. Some of these will have been anticipated and some will be in response to what is happening in real time.

All changes are made in the light of the course set and the place we are travelling towards.

This section therefore explores some of the elements that inform this journey and that makes for good pilotage. So let me bring this back to organisational life…

What is your change architecture?

One question I often ask the leaders of change programmes is 'What is the change architecture that is helping you scope the work and anticipate the decisions that need to be made during the through life of the programme?' In a significant percentage of cases the answer is 'we do not have an architecture beyond the project plan'.

This response and assessment is both honest and worrying. It also contributes to the high failure rate of change. It is the equivalent of trying to build a substantial house without architectural plans or even a picture in our mind's eye of what it might look like. Occasionally using this approach you may get a creative masterpiece of design. Usually you get something that is not fit for purpose.

> All changes are made in the light of the course set and the place we are travelling towards.

Figuring out what to do when and in what sequence is of critical importance.

Project and programme management skills are vital and along with this capability is required a deep understanding of the change process and transitional practice. This is an additional discipline and informs our ability to navigate successfully.

As I have asserted earlier, the call for leaders to be able to navigate in 'uncharted waters' is wholly dependent on them in the first instance being able to navigate. Navies around the world that are pushing the boundaries of technology are just beginning to figure this out.

As part of this figuring out – which to be honest we are all doing in these extraordinary times – I would argue that it is important to have a discipline and some structure to help organise our thinking in the fluidity in which we all find ourselves doing business.

What I see on the ground is that well over 50% of businesses have no such framework, as well as lacking navigational understanding and experience. The consequence is that leaders spend much of their time fire-fighting and working reactively, which in turn sets up a whole layer of consequential cost and inefficiencies.

In my book, 'Ensuring change delivers success' (Lever, 2017), I offer a practical overview of five important phases, and also explore the flow of activity and choices that reside in each of them. An increasing number of our customers take this overview and translate it into their own language, adding content and processes relevant to their organisations. This seems to help frame things and assist all involved to understand in more depth and breadth what should be happening when and in what sequence. The point really being that all change needs some kind of practical architecture whether it is the one I have outlined or not.

Making the first steps count

In the very early stages of implementation people will be 'reading' both the scripted and non-scripted messages and will have started to draw conclusions from what they are hearing. This information will be picked up from official communications, from the chain of management who inevitably will add their own interpretations, and of course, from the rumour mill. Get the narrative and the nature of the communication right and the shift will start to happen elegantly, as things slot into place in the right sequence. However if the early activities lack coherence and the start is haphazard resulting in an unexpected and bumpy ride, confidence will begin to be eroded. If this happens it will take effort to bring everything back on course –and this begins the additional expense of retrofitting and applying patches.

> **Leaving the dockside, manoeuvring and then heading out to sea has got to capitalise on the excitement of the voyage and not be interrupted by events that undermine the positive anticipation.**

If corrective action is taken early, the cost can be kept manageable but the longer the 'bumpiness' is allowed to persist, the higher the cost. All leaders should remember that once things have begun to run away and develop a momentum of their own, the true cost becomes systemic and consequential. One bad briefing or decision will cost, say, £1000 to correct. If this is not sorted adequately and a second bad decision is made on the back of the first, the cost could well escalate to £10,000. Fully loaded consequential costs can quickly cripple a change programme. In one council we calculated that the full cost of a poorly defined decision making process, and consequent hold-ups and the lost opportunities that resulted, was costing around

£250,000 in just one service area. There were seven service areas.

This is why the departure from the current state particularly in those initial first steps has to be done well as it sets the tone for the whole journey. Leaving the dockside, manoeuvring and then heading out to sea has got to capitalise on the excitement of the voyage and not be interrupted by events that undermine the positive anticipation. So I want my crew focused, alert, communicating, looking calm but on top of everything that can be under their control. I want to create an atmosphere of efficient and unobtrusive excellence.

Those first moments are just so important.

Make sure any shift is readable to all

If my voyage were to be tracked, it would describe many changes in direction and speed as we respond to and take advantage of a whole host of factors. At sea we also operate in a highly regulated environment with lots of traffic and potential sources of collisions. This traffic will be made up of our sister ships of the fleet, by competitors, and by a vast array of commercial vessels and pleasure craft. In order to avoid bumping into other vessels I have to, at all times, comply with the Regulations for the Prevention of Collisions at Sea. These are very technical but they are outworked in just three ways. We try and make all movements and shifts in position and speed (a) as early as we can; (b) deliberate and intentional; and (c) observable.

These fundamentally critical principles, outworked practically, underpin good seamanship. They instil confidence in crew, passengers and other vessels that all is well. By applying these rules (and they are rules, defined by official regulation) as well as common sense, we are also reducing potential confusion on our own vessel and on the bridges of those around us. In effect they communicate, 'we are under way, making way and under command'. All is well.

So how does a business translate this into practical effort?

Practical implications of the three principles

Making early movements

1 Seafarers hate having to take late and rushed decisions. Leaving things until the latest point where action can be taken often limits choice and, to restate again, choice is the currency of navigation. So early action gives us room to manoeuvre.

To make early movements any leader has to be first of all aware of what is going on before making decisions about direction and speed. There must, therefore, be multiple points in the operation where leaders collect and start to make sense of information that is being generated in real time. So along with financial information including revenue data and costs, I would expect to see, among other things:

- sales and marketing information;

- cultural information;

- change readiness assessments;

- data from managers around performance targets;

- data from HR about morale, staff turnover, current skill levels and what is required and being developed;

- current resilience of ICT and state of digital capability;

- information from the programmes or change team about status, and levels of change readiness;

- customer feedback;

- benchmark data;

- current status of information channels.

This all presupposes that there is an effective information collecting process embedded in the enterprise. Most importantly this needs to be reviewed on a regular basis as 'combined information' by a skilled and experienced team, that can make sense of the trends and shifts.

Picking up information early means that the team has to be very good at recognising patterns, spotting very subtle shifts, and also be able to combine strands of data to read the emergent messages. Along with this, managers need to relearn the simple art of walking around and chatting. And where the workforce is working flexibly and in multiple sites this means visits, Skype calls and face-time sessions. There has to be an emphasis on connectivity and thinking and 'reading' emerging information, together.

Deliberate and intentional

2 Working with intention requires us to be making good and well-timed decisions based on data, knowledge, insight and some wisdom. When put under any kind of scrutiny we need to be able to explain why this decision was made and what was the hoped-for outcome. Of course we may not get all of these decisions right, but the process needs to be deliberate and timely. The decisions we make and take represent the area where we are going to be held accountable. As has been

said before (several times!), navigation is about making decisions.

It is at this point many organisations then are faced with a dilemma. Because of the significant breadth of decisions that have to be made across the entire enterprise, senior leaders figure out that they don't have the time or the bandwidth to answer and decide on everything. So many reach for the 'empowerment solution'- it makes sense...

And here reside two traps:

1. Saying that all are empowered but in practice retaining most of the decisions in a centralised group or with just one individual, causes much frustration as time increases and quality goes down. It undermines confidence in leaders and the management chain.

2. Devolving everything throughout the business without clear boundaries causes chaos at best and anarchy at worst.

Both of these very common approaches will cause pain and disruption and some will end in disaster.

Going back to the principle of intentionality – this particularly resides in how decisions are made and taken. So there is an option 3...

The leadership needs to figure out what decisions, (based on content, exposure, magnitude and customer impact) are made by whom, who needs to be involved and who needs visibility. Everyone needs to be very clear about levels of responsibility, accountability and authority. Even having done this there will be overlaps, anomalies and grey areas, which need to be anticipated and escalation routes and procedures put in place. By practically investing time in sorting this all out before 'engines are engaged', confidence in the system is bolstered along with clarity.

Observable

3 At sea it is so important that all of our actions are observable and readable to all other vessels and our own crew. This reduces ambiguity and potential confusion. So a change of course or a change in speed, if done early enough, will signal our intent as long as everyone can see what we are doing.

Businesses are no different and those successful at bringing in reform or transformation take this principle and build it into the fabric of 'how things are done around here'. In the Unipart HQ in Oxford any visitor is struck by the visual impact of customer comments and insights, progress reports, the tricky issues still being worked on, successes and stellar performances – all displayed in reception and in the corridors and canteens.

B&Q had their 'rich picture' in places that staff would pass through or meet in and therefore could see – they were big, bold and expressed in B&Q language. The orange room where projects were displayed visually along with all of the questions that were currently being worked on supported this picture of the journey.

In one Oxfordshire council each Service publicly displayed performance points that became the focus for positive conversations between members of the service and between different service areas. Meetings were held with this up to date information used as the backdrop. Progress and key events coming up were literally in everyone's line of vision during conversations.

Smart organisations make as much information as possible as visible as possible and keep it accurate and up to date. This simple practice reduces confusion and confirms to all who need to know what is going on and that the journey is progressing well.

From here to there

If the gap between where we are currently and where we would like to be has any significant distance – and if there is any degree of complexity to the journey – then we know that the route will not be in a straight line. If tracked the headings will go this way and that as choices are made although the overall course setting will at all times pull toward the intended destination.

At sea the course we set, the direction we head in and the bearings we travel along are subject to many factors. Even in open sea there will be moments when we will change direction for a variety of reasons.

The size of the gap between where we are and where we would like to be also has profound implications, including fuel requirements and rates of usage, provisions required, supply lines, and managing customer expectations/enhancing their experience. All of this has a cost attached and the bigger the gap the more investment will be required both up front and during the voyage. This equally applies to organisations who would be wise to figure out the fully loaded investment cost before setting off on the change.

There will be times when we on the bridge will be restricted to the navigation channels that are deep enough to travel along through shallow waters and between the sandbanks that surround us. These channels are subject to both the Rules for the Prevention of Collisions at Sea and local traffic laws, so my behaviour whilst in these shipping channels is highly regulated.

In open water I am still governed by the collision regulations, and by operational considerations such as my estimated time of arrival, factoring in weather implications, sea conditions, how much fuel my owners are prepared for me to burn, any known hazards and the availability of dock space when we arrive. All of this makes up the plan for the journey.

And then of course there are all of the 101 things that are happening in the real world, such as other vessels not observing the rules, pirates hijacking vessels, sailing regattas that impede passage and military manoeuvres, to name just a few. This contributes to the off-plan activity that translates into the various decisions that have to be made.

Both the on-plan and off-plan work informs choices that a captain and crew are continually making. To re-state:

It's all about choices...

At sea the guiding principle is to make choices in good time and make them definitive and observable enough so that intent is always clear to other vessels. Some of this other traffic will be required by maritime law to change direction and speed if they are the vessel 'giving way'.

/// **Smart organisations make as much information as possible as visible as possible and keep it accurate and up to date.**

If these other ships fail to respond, particularly if they are required to give way, I will sound five short blasts on the ship's horn. This in essence says 'I have no idea at this point what your intention is and you are required to respond. But for my part I am maintaining speed and course'. If this fails to get a response, a call on the radio will follow. If necessary I will take action to avoid a collision or other situation, even when it's not my responsibility to change heading and speed. This latter action is a judgement call that is finely balanced. If I change heading too early it may confuse other vessels that could be just late in responding to the situation and this in turn can create more risk.

If action is left too late, even though I might be technically within my rights to maintain my heading, being hit by what should be the giving-way vessel neither makes my actions right nor renders me immune to prosecution. I would have to justify my decisions as a seaman to a board of enquiry. And these are scary places made up of former and practising captains who enjoy taking things apart!

If I am the giving-way vessel, I am required to take early, definite and observable action to reduce speed or change my heading. Last minute corrections and changes tend to end up panicking everyone on board and scaring the crew on other vessels. In the main we all prefer calm responses even if this eventually has to be done at speed.

So if anyone were tracking my progress, every change in direction would be informed by a choice I was making at this time. People who have relevant information and insights to contribute will always inform these choices. I have learned long ago that a single view or perspective, even if it is from the captain or CEO, has many blind spots. Collaboration is essential.

This is the very essence of Navigational Principle 3.

The basics
Back to organisational life...

Once the current location is known across a range of dimensions and the leaders have begun to get a handle on the intended destination, the next stage is to figure out the practical actions required to get there. There will always be several options around the preferred route so this does come back to making a judgement call.

The difference between the current reality and the intended destination will determine how big a shift will be needed. Simply put, the size of the gap is rather important.

In navigational terms this is called the range and, to be clear, range has to be assessed against many components of the total operation. It may look from just the financial viewpoint as though shifts can be made without huge investment. However, the shift in behaviour from, say, a directive leadership culture to one that is based on collaboration may be enormous – and require significant support and money to make sure new behaviours become part of the 'reworked way things are done around here'.

Bridging the gap takes time, effort and money
The size of the gap is just so critical to assess as it will also determine how much time, effort and money will be required to make the journey. It also defines what specifically needs to be done in terms of both tasks and the 'people' dimension. All of this should be built into the cost of the programme but it also represents an investment that gives the change programme the very best chance of delivering. I know I have repeated this principle several times – it's just that in the reality of organisational life many change programmes are resourced inadequately.

In the real world many things get in the way of efforts to equip programmes adequately enough to succeed. Executives don't give enough time, the day job gets in

the way, the finance department withholds funding or has miscalculated what is available, there is little contingency funding, decision making is slow and confused... and the list could go on. This is why the success rate of change that fully delivers intended benefits is so low. Some leaders, who think they can get away with any of the above and prove to be the exception, find out pretty quickly that they can't.

At sea, if I know the voyage is going to take 10,000 gallons of fuel with a reserve of 50% I would not cast off with 7,500 gallons in my fuel tank. Nor should any business.

In organisations this gap, and therefore cost, will be across multiple dimensions and disciplines. The more tangible elements, such as restructuring, introducing new IT platforms, work-flow analysis, vendor buying agreements and figuring out required sales margins, are relatively straightforward to cost. It is the more intangible elements like cultural and behavioural patterns that are much more complex to articulate and measure.

This has to be done however, because we know from the research that culture is the single most influential determinant of change success (Atticus, n.d.). If it is that important we have to be able to articulate what it is and be able to measure it in some way. Jim Collins describes in his book 'Good to great and the social sectors' (2006) how this can practically be done with the application of creativity and discipline.

The required repetition of new behaviours takes time and also has a price tag
We know from the latest findings coming out of research in neuroscience, that 'rewiring' patterned behaviour can also be done but time and much repetition are required to embed the new ways. So the good news for individuals and organisations is that 'plasticity' provides the hope of real behavioural change. The bad news for some managers is that the 'new behaviours' have to be repeated time and time again for them to become habit and constitute the new pattern. For those leaders who believe that you 'tell them once' and after that everyone should just get on with change and forget about all of the 'people' stuff, this is very challenging news.

However if repetition does not happen... nor will the change. It really is that straightforward.

The shift
Once all of the gap analysis has been completed across a range of dimensions including various geographies and business functions, this is then understood through the various lenses of:

- strategic ambition;

- the law and regulations;

- the business operation;

- employees;

- wider stakeholders;

- supply chains;

- customers;

- shareholders.

Out of this diagnostic information will flow all of the multiple projects that begin to make up the plan for 'what happens when... and in what sequence... and with what dependencies'. So this is a lot of work before implementation starts. What employees notice, however, is not so much all of the preparation activity above, but when stuff starts to 'go live' and when it begins to affect them and their customers directly.

> // There are some change initiatives which have been so inadequately thought through that they should be resisted or at least be tested very strongly.

Of course, all of this is outworked during the transition when, for the first part of the journey at least, people will still be looking back towards how it used to be. The focus only shifts when enough of the population accepts (either enthusiastically or reluctantly) that the future is different from the past. This is helped if the 'why are we changing' and 'where are we going to?' questions have compelling answers.

At the point of 'letting go', which is at the bottom of the transition curve, people know that they have to change and the focus shifts from the past to what the future might mean for them. How quickly employees get to this point is subject to a number of factors. Smart organisations invest in supporting their workforce through these initial phases, not least because, as I have mentioned, it is cheaper to get it right first time than have to retrofit patches and mop up messes caused by poorly thought through comments at the staff briefings.

Resistance
Up until that moment when enough of the workforce starts to accept a new future, there may well be various groups and mind-sets that remain opposed to the change and will be trying to undermine efforts to do things

differently. This pretty much always occurs to a greater or lesser extent. It happens even if the change makes sense and offers a compelling reason to leave the current location and even if it proposes a compelling glimpse of a desired future. However...

There are some change initiatives which have been so inadequately thought through that they should be resisted or at least be tested very strongly.

In one such example, happening as I write, the Customer Service Director of a council is trying to digitalise the customer experience. Her solution, which includes introducing new platforms and vendors, is 'IT madness' according to the ICT head and team. They know that this approach by someone who is not IT savvy will end up costing more and will have enraged the customers. Currently the voices of the experts are described as being obstructive and change resistant – although the reality is that they are trying to help. I wonder what it is going to take for the Customer Services Director to take a look up from her dogma and start listening to those who know a thing or two about what is technically and financially possible.

In this and many other situations resistance could well be a useful wake-up call that may impact either the way the change is being handled, or indeed the end destination. At least it has the potential to start a more robust conversation about the way ahead. This takes time, money and effort to sort out and poses yet more choices for the leadership to ponder and decide on. In the example just given I wonder where the CEO is, as his voice feels absent.

Change is particularly vulnerable at the start of any programme. The race is often about establishing a narrative that has some traction early on. A good friend of mine remarked that if the rumours are more believable than the stuff being pushed out by the communications team, then the change will be dead in the water.

The strategy which answers the question 'how are we going to get there' needs to take account of all of the above.

The plan and preparation for off-plan events
So figuring out 'how are we going to get there...?' has two fundamental parts.

The plan
There is a need for a comprehensive and robust plan, plus plausible scenarios that consider the 'what if' questions that will form the basis of the programme of work. If done well, the debates and mutual 'thinking together' will drive out much of the unknown. This is

where a collaborative and collective effort, engaging foresight, is of key interest and importance to all leaders, programme managers and members of the change team.

A clear strategy of escalation and decision making needs to be authorised, put in place and communicated to all, which will manage all of the off-plan events.

In military terms no plan is likely to exist unaltered much beyond the first shots of battle. However this does not negate the need to plan. Figuring out what to do and when, and how the various activities and projects fit together, is critical. It is in the debates with a range of stakeholders and the destruction-testing playing with the 'what if' questions that thinking is shaped and formed. It is wise for leaders to invite some key trusted colleagues who are not afraid to give counter-points to be part of this group. This team could well be the start of the programme management office (PMO) or change team.

By employing techniques such as systems thinking and scenario planning, and by modelling the way, the vagaries of the unknown can be reduced. Simply put all of these activities are encouraging, informed, insightful and intelligent foresight.

Going off-plan

If the above has been done well, the amount of surprises over the lifespan of the programme will have been reduced. However there will still be surprises and they can come from some very unexpected sources. For example:

- a staff briefing that says the wrong thing or says something different from last time;

- a reduction in funding;

- increased staff turnover rates suddenly going through the ceiling;

- forgetting to put VAT on building material;

- the CEO falling out with the chairperson;

- officers not involving members fully enough;

- a change in taxation practice;

- the introduction of a new mandatory regulation;

- poor summer weather that reduces the sale of outdoor equipment, which in turn reduces like for like sales by 10%.

These are all things that will affect the organisation's ability to deliver the change. What is therefore needed

at the start is a clear strategy of engagement and communication that can respond to the squalls that crop up, which could slow progress or in extreme cases capsize the whole ship.

The demand for certainty, and the reality

In the search for absolute certainty, some still ask and demand to know how exactly we are going to get there and what the precise plan of action is.

This is a totally fair point of view and if I were in control of everything and knew everything I would be able to answer it. This is not a message that some people and some political bodies want to hear, though. But the plan itself has got to go a fair way to answering these demands without falling into the trap of setting false expectations. There is much we don't know and can't possibly know.

This makes a call on leaders in regard to how honest they might want to be and need to be on this. And this comes back to culture and particularly the underpinning values around openness, and honesty that guide the organisation and the leader(s). It should be noted that almost everyone believes in honesty and openness the critical questions, however, are to what extent and how much. In other words the boundaries and limits that we all habitually place around things being said and shared, is of great interest and importance.

Trying to get as much certainty as possible

As a navigator I would have my plan for the voyage. I would set my course with waymarks dividing up the journey. I would have worked out distances, course changes and known decision points where I could go this way or that depending on real-time conditions. I would have worked out fuel required and made sure I had a reserve in case the sea conditions changed or I had to go around a nasty weather front. Much thought would have gone into the plan with many people involved in its creation.

We would have considered weather forecasts, tide tables, refuelling points, and so on. We would also make sure that the vessel and crew were all compliant with the heavily regulated world we worked in. I would also need my crew to know how I expected them to behave and where they were empowered to make their professional calls. Each of us would need to have a clarity of role that included who was responsible for what, who was accountable for what and to whom, and most importantly who was authorised to make what decisions. All of this we could be clear about, in order to work the plan and schedules but respond intelligently to the other stuff that goes on at sea which is outside our sphere of influence.

A plan is simply that

At sea we will be affected by weather fronts not behaving

as predicted, which then sets off other decisions about heading, speed and estimated time of arrival. Course resets have an implication for fuel consumption, which directly impacts profits. I can go faster on a longer route to avoid a particular bout of bad weather and get passengers/cargo to the port on time but burn up a lot more fuel. Or I can take a longer route, go slower and not meet my ETA. This won't burn excessive fuel but it will burn the patience of passengers or those waiting for cargo and that has a direct cost too. In the main I tended to opt to get passengers to where they needed to be on time. But I did get gentle reprimands from time to time about my fuel consumption.

Heavy traffic in restricted channels will have an impact... A distress call from another vessel will need to be responded to... Passengers and crew being struck down by seasickness or some other condition all make for interesting voyages.

So you have your plan ... but then you need to respond and/or not respond to everything else. Every decision that is made has consequences and sets in motion another series of decisions. Many 'incidents' at sea happen as a result of an escalating series of events with increasing consequences, which taken as a whole sometimes end in disaster, though each event looked at on its own may not have appeared too significant.

Knowing and doing are not the same

Most people in business do grasp this distinction and understand the message of the metaphor. When in conversation I have explained this in some detail, leaders will often nod in agreement saying they get the point. However, too many times we see the reality of how change programmes are delivered. Leaders often agree in principle with much of what has been said so far but then seemingly ignore the fact that this all needs to be practically outworked.

It would be utter madness to set off to sea without sufficient fuel for the voyage. Yet so many change programmes set off in a flurry without fully understanding or costing the journey to be made. One senior leadership team overseeing a really significant merger and far-reaching changes was only prepared to invest in meeting every six weeks. They had delegated the change to an inexperienced programme management officer and a change team hired from the retail industry for their customer handling skills, but none of this team had never been involved in a change programme. In my opinion this was totally reckless behaviour.

There can be pressure from some stakeholders to ignore the principles underpinning effective change leadership, because they hope to get lucky or don't see the importance of them. So the path between point A and point B is still drawn as a straight line with a sequential

set of project steps (Figure 4). This is particularly observable in organisations with any degree of political oversight and membership. Politicians want certainty and to be able to demonstrate they have fixed the issue, as election time comes around far too quickly. Understandably they have to be able to answer their inquisitors when asked 'so what are you doing precisely on this matter?' and 'what have you actually achieved?' Trying to explain to a duplicitous press or a public not too interested in the difference between planned and off-plan responses, that projects and programmes and events appear and weren't on the radar because they were unknown unknowns... is difficult!

Perhaps some honesty from all sectors is needed?

/// So you have your plan ... but then you need to respond and/or not respond to everything else. Every decision that is made has consequences and sets in motion another series of decisions.

The difference between projects and programmes

There is a tendency for some businesses just to treat the plan with its many projects of work as one glorified single project. This tendency seems to increase if time pressures are all consuming. Projects and programmes look similar on the surface but are very different in reality.

A financial director of a large local authority told me that programme management was just the latest invention and scam on the part of business consultants to get more work and 'up their fees'. He failed to see that all of the work that was currently being done by many teams and services under *his* leadership had no controls, no oversight and was about to come crashing in on everyone. He resolutely dismissed any notion of pinch points on resources or trying to understand the interconnectedness of his organisation. His failure to accept anything that wasn't in his small box of understanding caused major issues across the authority. His total disregard for any of his colleagues' views pointed to a lack of emotional intelligence at best whilst some regarded the behaviour as simply arrogant. Sadly, some individuals and some teams are just beyond help.

In practical terms I would expect to be able to go to the programmes room where I could see how all of the projects going on throughout the organisation over a period of time connected with each other. At a glance I would be able to see pinch points, resourcing strategies, interdependencies, who was involved in what, end dates, slippage points, consequences and the rest. This information would be displayed visually and would be very readable and accessible to all.

Complex change requires an organisation's best people to be involved at all stages of the change. Sadly we see some organisations use simply 'available' people to steer the change and the result is as predictable as it is painful for all.

Successful implementation also requires a highly capable and experienced team of project managers, and above them programme managers, to help deliver on behalf of the leadership. (Programmes are usually made up of a bundle of interdependent projects.) The project management community needs to be experienced enough to withstand the pressures to deliver quickly that will be brought to bear on them by leaders and other stakeholders. They need to have tough skins and be politically savvy enough to engage with stakeholders who are driven by many different forms of ambition.

A question that is often asked is whether the programme management officers (PMOs) really need to understand change, as surely it's merely about managing a programme of work. My answer is that PMOs do indeed need to have a deep understanding of the change and transition process in addition to their core discipline. Navigating the change process is a complex task, which requires specific experience and knowledge. This is the reason I have illustrated the three principles of navigation to show that there is more to the process than perhaps it seems at first sight.

It is rare for leaders to be trained and assessed in navigational practice. However, given what we know is happening in Digital Transformation I

suspect that we will all need to update our understanding of change before too long, or like the US navy rediscover the core principles underlying the technology.

What follows is a case in point. Most say that they understand that the journey, and therefore the plan, does not represent a single straight line of action from point A to point B. They tell you they know that the path features choices that require good and timely answers. This often requires a change in heading or some other

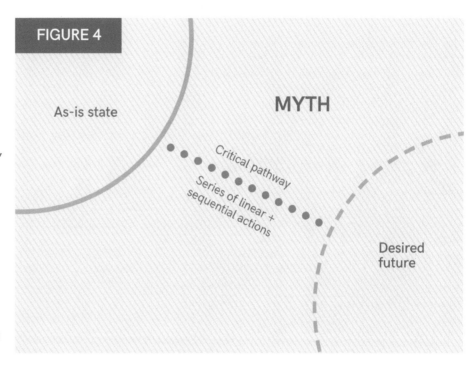

FIGURE 4

As-is state

MYTH

Critical pathway

Series of linear + sequential actions

Desired future

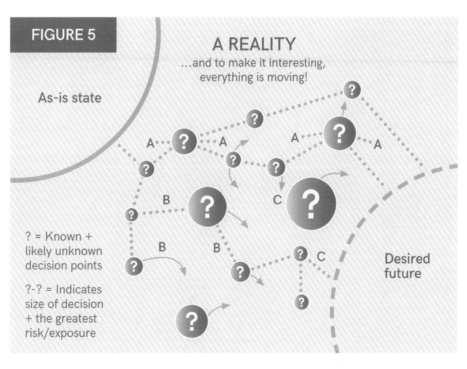

FIGURE 5

As-is state

A REALITY
...and to make it interesting, everything is moving!

? = Known + likely unknown decision points

?-? = Indicates size of decision + the greatest risk/exposure

Desired future

readjustment. And yet despite this much pressure will be brought to bear on the change team to work in a linear 'step by step' fashion. So despite the acknowledgement of the above, the programme takes on a mechanistic feel, providing a false sense of certainty and control and ignoring the clear places where choices are still yet to be made.

The myth

For the 'straight line' enthusiasts and those who have been pressurised into the step by step approach the change picture created looks like Figure 4.

This illusion can fool people into thinking the process is all very straightforward. Sadly this linear approach wins votes and breeds false confidence that everything is in hand, but in the main it comes unravelled when the wind changes, when the price of fuel goes up, or when a technology doesn't do what the sales team said it would.

> // From everything we know, figuring out priorities has to involve people from multiple standpoints, as it is difficult for just one person or even a limited number of executives to have the whole picture

The reality

The reality, of course, is rather more like Figure 5.

Route A is the planned course and routes B and C are the contingency routes if... these are based on plausible scenarios kicking in. Of course, there will be other alternatives.

Here we are looking down on the overall territory, but to a leader and leadership teams it will look a bit more like Figure 6 as they stare into the future.

This can all seem rather intimidating and confusing as it poses the question of what priority choices have to be made in what order. From everything we know, figuring out priorities has to involve people from multiple standpoints, as it is difficult for just one person or even a limited number of executives to have the whole picture. Multiple perspectives are critical to figuring out the priorities in the complex and systemic world we live and trade in.

One of the assertions I made at the beginning of this book was that although people use the terminology of navigation the application indicates a shallow understanding of the principles. So for example, leaders that I have taken through the above content and who have said that it has been really useful... still articulate a change as decribed in Figure 7.

The issue with the pathway is that it still doesn't fully represent the full range of options open to the leader. Its scope is too narrow. It is already defining what is possible in a restricted way. So, being blunt.... the plan is only just a little more sophisticated than the one shown in Figure 4.

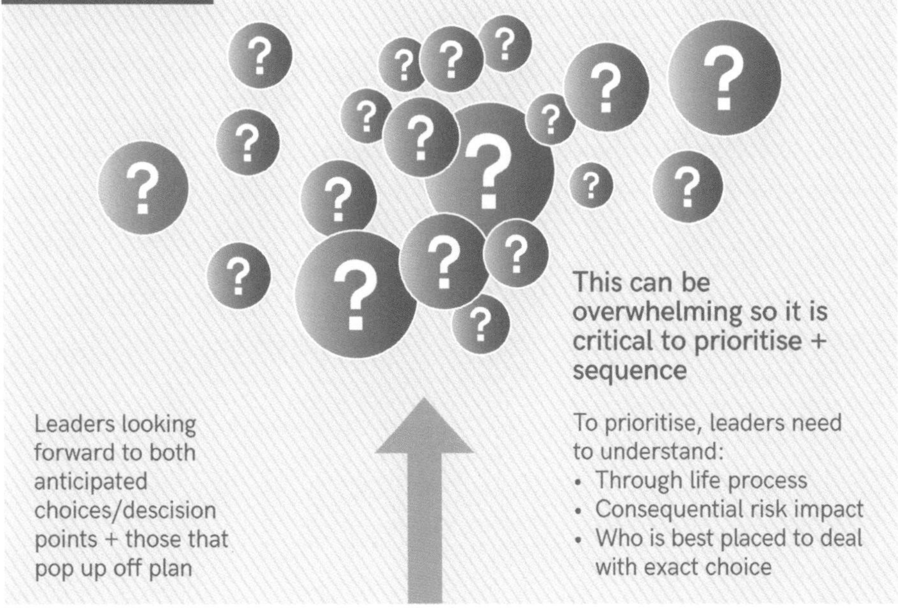

As already stated, setting off for any future destination will mean that we enter the territory of the unknown and have to deal with stuff outside of our control. Some leaders however use this as an excuse when a change programme goes wrong, by glibly saying that 'hindsight is a wonderful thing'. The truth is that these leaders for a variety of reasons didn't apply foresight anywhere near enough. In my own experience something like 60-70% of the failure of change programmes is perfectly describable, knowable and therefore predictable before the process starts. In many situations, something we know as PPP (pretty poor planning... or words to that effect!) prevails.

Poor navigators make an inadequate plan and then get caught off guard by something that in their world was

FIGURE 6

Leaders looking forward to both anticipated choices/descision points + those that pop up off plan

This can be overwhelming so it is critical to prioritise + sequence

To prioritise, leaders need to understand:
• Through life process
• Consequential risk impact
• Who is best placed to deal with exact choice

unexpected but which many people were pointing out and saying had to be factored in before implementation. They then excuse themselves by saying 'only hindsight is an exact science'. They fail to grasp that the knowledge that could have ensured success was there all along in the organisation or in the sector.

It is my contention that much more is knowable at the start of the programme than seems at first sight. There are ways to find this information and build it in to our preparation. What this effort is trying to do is reduce the cone of uncertainty as in Figure 8 below.

If the culture of the organisation is Change-Able (open, mission orientated and relational, has a can-do attitude and brings together people to problem solve) this helps to create a free flow of information. Overlaying this with disciplines like 'systems thinking' which views an enterprise as a joined up whole with end to end processes or 'scenario planning' based on understanding the rules of the game, key 'knowns and unknowns', creating plausible scenarios which kick in when the reality on the ground becomes clearer... is vital to give a plan robustness and flexibility.

Chantell Ilbury and Clem Sunter's book 'Mind of a fox' (2001) is an excellent example of how scenario thinking is both practical and vital for preparing for complex shifts. 'Modelling the way' is another example of how a process that combines creativity and discipline can reduce some of the unknowns. The ability to build mock-up models in the real and/or virtual worlds in order to answer some of the 'what if' questions has underpinned so many advancements of our recent experience including the introduction of the 747 airliner, bringing Apollo 13 back to earth and the UK's Crossrail project.

Whether it is through systems thinking, scenario planning or modelling the way, the activity is all about reducing uncertainty by figuring out what we know and don't know. This is illustrated in Figure 8 where by looking ahead with

foresight the 'cone of uncertainty' can be reduced and 'possibility' increased.

Extraordinarily though, few in business use the approach outside of training workshops.

Off-plan responses
Of course information changes over the lifespan of a programme as well as off-plan events happening, so the operating plan, which will be an amalgam of projects, will

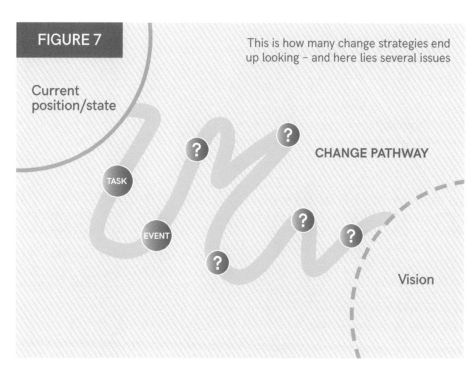

FIGURE 7

This is how many change strategies end up looking – and here lies several issues

Current position/state

TASK

EVENT

? ? ? ? ?

CHANGE PATHWAY

Vision

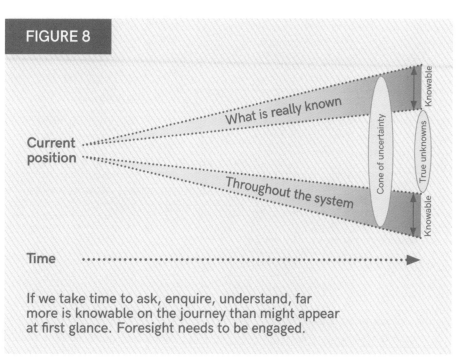

FIGURE 8

Current position

What is really known

Throughout the system

Cone of uncertainty

True unknowns

Knowable

Knowable

Time

If we take time to ask, enquire, understand, far more is knowable on the journey than might appear at first glance. Foresight needs to be engaged.

also need to flex and shift to some extent. As a leader you have to be totally involved with the brief and plan, as this will take on a life of its own. The process always ends up in decisions being taken in the real world and often about off-plan events. You can only do this if the leadership is tight, open and meets regularly. A relationally dysfunctional leadership trying to figure out off-plan responses will normally create confusion and disaster. So sorting out relationships so that they can work with focus and some elegance is enormously important.

This will become even more critical when Artificially Intelligent (AI) systems start to make autonomous decisions. So along with a need for a clear regulatory framework, responses in this very different world we are seeing emerge, have to be talked about before everything goes live. Again processes like scenario planning that ask plausible 'what if' questions will be of central importance. If Digital Transformation delivers speed, then responses to off-plan events will need to happen fast, as well. I hope that leaders figure this out before any disasters happen.

It is for all of these reasons that a simple project approach to change will be insufficient where there is any degree of complexity. The reality will be a change process with bundles of projects that should fit within an overall programme framework. The programme management office or the change team often oversees this and has the authority to respond in good time.

The programmes room
Figuring out how projects fit together and align allows everyone to identify resourcing blocks and resource requirements. This has consequences for review of progress and setting realistic end dates. Creating momentum and a feeling of progress is all important, as we have asserted more than once in this book; and it is critical to see ahead of time where there could be impediments to progress.

Change of any significant size should have a 'programmes area' with all of the projects visually represented, so that at a glance everyone can see the extent of the work, current status, its fit, progress being made and where all the projects are going to demand support from IT or HR or from the communications team. Visually the pinch points and resourcing issues become obvious as do end dates and key deliverables. In B&Q they called this 'the orange room'. This significant office space was open to all employees and:

- displayed information;

- was a place of listening to concerns;

- encouraged information exchange;

- asked great and unfiltered questions;

- displayed answers and performance points;

- was where the programme plan was made public;

- was where all the amendments and learnings on route were captured.

It was here everything was democratised and ownership shifted from leaders to the people.

At sea I may change direction as part of the plan or I may respond to off-plan events and situations. At times I may push hard ahead and in rough weather I will need to reduce speed and ride out a storm. In all of this the intended destination is an ever-present pull. In other words I may shift direction; I may even have to turn about for a period but I never lose sight of where we are going unless of course the destination itself becomes impossible to reach and then we may have to consider alternatives.

Choice is governed by need, values, regulations and protocols
What governs any shifts in direction and speed contains both the pragmatic and the underpinning values that shape choices. In the collision regulations there is an elegant rule for all masters, which says in summary, 'If in the event that none of these rules apply to your situation you are required to do the right thing. At all times good seamanship shall prevail.'

Some organisations have an ethical code that runs through all decision making. This is explored more fully in the book, Ethical ambition, by Derrick Bell (2002).

The example of how a pharmaceutical company closed down its UK operation with its values to the fore has already been mentioned. The pragmatic reality was the business was unable to sustain this operation but they chose with real courage to look after everyone in the process of closure. Their values became more prominent and even more relevant to them in the tough times.

In Collins and Porras's (1996) work on vision and strategy, published through the Harvard Business Review, the authors emphasise the point that how an organisation lives its values and beliefs is just as important as the stated destination. Jim Collins, author of 'Good to great' (2001), makes the assertion that values are more important than vision. I think he overstates this, but the two combined are vital components of successful change.

You find out what is a true value when under pressure
It's often under the pressure of change that everyone finds out what the real values of the organisation actually are. When experienced positively these are the operating rules that govern how the plan is implemented, breathing life into choices. Good seamanship as required by the collision

regulations is about compliance, but with common sense and good values running through it.

Whist at sea I was fortunate to work for a company founded by a skilled shipwright and entrepreneur who came from humble beginnings. He built his fleet of ferries on some basic values:

- Expect and help people to perform well.

- Reward hard work.

- Have fun.

- Treat all with respect.

- Spot talent and develop.

- Practice and practice and then repeat again.

- Keep on top of the detail.

- Most of all let your eyes do the work and read what is going on now and figure out what will take place later (Figure 8).

Simple stuff – it was never written down but it was lived.

When he extended the business, taking incredible personal and financial risks, the values were still the same. Intense pressure and stress, which almost killed him one winter as he oversaw the completion of a new vessel, did not affect the way he behaved or how he expected all his employees to behave. But he was also savvy enough to hire people whose values already aligned more or less with his. He figured that getting the hiring decisions right first time would save time, money and a great deal of unwanted hassle.

Many times we have observed that even with a little additional pressure in a system, values become forgotten or revealed for what they truly are – just words on paper. In the vagaries of implementation with its heading corrections, times of going fast and slow as conditions dictate, pausing to get bearings, it is the organisation's values that have the potential to be the consistent and stabilising force.

Values guide how we relate to others and how we make and take decisions, dictate how honest we are and where we put personal and operational boundaries. Values have the potential to bring our behaviour back from the craziness of our world to the authentic core.

If ever you are not sure what to do … do the right thing. A principle of seamanship enshrined in regulation

The Regulations for the Prevention of Collision at Sea govern pretty near everything that goes on. The one rule that holds everything together is the rule demanding good seamanship at all times. There is the same requirement on all leaders, in whatever context and market they are operating.

If as a captain I fail to live up to this rule, any enquiry will quite rightly hold me to account. I wish this were so in organisations as well, where I see far too many failed leaders being promoted, given special projects and rewarded for failure. How is this possible?

Of course the 15-20% of leaders who do navigate change successfully and deliver great outcomes should be the ones given recognition and reward for these represent the Change-Able leadership identified by the Atticus (n.d.) research.

> I may even have to turn about for a period but I never lose sight of where we are going–unless of course the destination itself becomes impossible to reach and then we may have to consider alternatives.

And finally it's all about the people

All of the words written in this book are fundamentally about people and how we honour effort and the lives that most invest in their work. Klaus Schwab of the WEF asserts (2015) that 'technology is made by people for people'.

Wise organisations and wise leaders know this and whilst we can never guarantee jobs and will have to take tough decisions on occasion we should all remember that we are impacting lives. How we support employees and customers will not only signal our values but will also determine medium and long term success. Anyone can do a hatchet job and leave ugly stumps and a devastated landscape but it takes care and skill to prune trees and bushes to create the productive and pleasant garden that most want to spend their futures in.

At sea the vessel moving through waves and wind has a distinctive sound if everything technological and mechanical is working well. This is amplified and added to if the 'sound' of crew and passengers is harmonious and good natured. In business this is described by the Atticus (n.d.) research as being 'Change-Able'.

Summary

In change there has to be a well thought through and robustly tested plan, which includes a plausible number of responses to likely scenarios.

When the plan proves incomplete or is impacted by events a previously constructed escalation procedure for decision making will kick in. If the leadership has delegated the change programme to the PMO the latter will need open access to all key decision makers.

As has already been stated, the route from A to B is rarely if ever a straight line.

All decisions set off other consequences throughout the system. It appears that fixing one thing can have a negative and escalating impact elsewhere if the whole is not viewed as an integrated end to end process.

Failure can be a great teacher. Using the excuse of 'hindsight being a wonderful thing' can simply be an excuse for inadequate preparation.

> **The values that guide Change-Able decision making should be operational not only in the good times but also (and most importantly) when things get difficult and fractious.**

From my own observation around 70% of the causes of failure can be identified before a programme starts (Figure 8).

The quality of the PMO or change team, both in capability and capacity terms, is vital. This team should be made up of an organisation's very best people and not those who are simply available.

Anything other than a simple change will require a programmes approach and discipline.

We advise that a programmes room is established and this should be open to all.

The values that guide Change-Able decision making should be operational not only in the good times but also (and most importantly) when things get difficult and fractious.

Everyone will discover what the true values of the organisation are when things don't go to plan.

Every decision has to be made with an eye to what is actually going on and where you are trying to get to, and should be informed by an overarching change strategy. We suggest an example in the book 'What happens when' (Lever, 2017) but whether this is adopted or not, it is critical to have a blueprint that governs movement between the key phases.

Some questions

- Is there a plan which all have confidence in?

- Have you realistically assessed your organisation's PMO capability? Does this team have the experience, understanding and proximity to leadership to deliver?

- Would you be able to take me to the programmes room (or virtual equivalent) so that I could see in an instant the current state of things, including what is being learnt, live questions being considered, successes and all future resource pinch points across the projects?

- To what extent has your organisation destruction-tested the plan and played with various plausible scenarios?

- How are you making progress with key stakeholders who may have different requirements of the change either operationally or politically? Therefore what is your stakeholder engagement strategy?

- Are your senior leaders open enough with each other to allow robust and open conversations? How do you know?

- Consider that awkward senior leader who asks the uncomfortable question standing alone in their view – is this person's voice truly welcome or just seen as a pain? (It could be they are just blocking, but it also could represent the wisdom required of the situation.)

- What approaches like systems thinking, scenario planning or modelling the way do you use to reduce some of the future uncertainty?

- Do you have waymarks identified, with regard to what tasks are anticipated when, and what emotions are likely to be swirling around when?

- Are the escalation routes clear and mature enough to respond to off-plan events in a timely manner?

- In what ways are the values of the organisation being lived on a daily basis and how are these informing the decision making/taking process?

- Do you have a clear understanding of the decision priorities and associated timescales?

Bringing together the key themes of this section and concluding remarks

At the heart of this section is the ability of leaders to think together and collectively feel the future journey, reducing uncertainty. This translates into robust plans that are rooted in the real world and delivered by the very best people who are aware, connected and authorised to be as agile as they need to be.

Not everything will go to plan however but maintaining momentum is critical. Speed though is not constant and there will be times when the programme will move at a fast pace and other times when things will be slower. But to repeat… momentum is everything.

Leadership

To lead means to navigate, to steer, to find good passage and to go somewhere. It requires a journey and willing followers who take up their own leadership opportunities so leadership becomes leaderships.

Leaders make a difference. It really is that simple, but whether that difference is positive or not depends on many factors. At the very heart of all activity, it is about creating the right conditions and culture for people to excel and then setting direction and skillfully steering toward it. At these times there might be a tendency to look for the new super version of leadership. I suspect if we go down this route we will find, as we always have, that supposed super leaders become villains once their 'sell by date' has been reached. In the future I hope we have a much more enlightened conversation about what we need from our leaders.

Waymarks to navigate this section

It is leaders who make the three principles of navigation come alive

The next couple of decades will feature vast changes in how we live, work, lead and indeed are prepared to be led. This will come from multiple shifts including:

- the climate;

- our security situation;

- our energy use;

- food production;

- Digital Transformation; and AI

- biological / medical advances;

- financial shifts;

- changes in political power structures;

- changes within society itself.

Who knows how much of the change will truly be disruptive, but I suspect more than we perhaps anticipate. Much of it will be positive and some of it will be of the more challenging variety. I do take note of Dr Stephen Hawkins' (2016) views that are troubling and provide an interesting counterpoint.

Taking the theme of Digital Transformation, one of my colleagues, Ross Harling, an EU business adviser, former European CIO of a tech giant and serial innovator, says in an unpublished article, 'A footnote for the future' (2017b):

'As we write, the world has already begun another era of unparalleled technological change, known as the "4th Industrial Revolution". This time taking place with information & communication technologies, rather than steel & coal.

"Digital Transformation" is being used to describe how this breadth of new capabilities will precipitate economic & social disruptions to current business models and operating procedures, as well as to customer & employee relationships. And it affects both Public and Commercial organisations, of all sizes and locations'.

The speed at which this is taking place means organisations need to become even better at adapting to new ways of working, particularly as their transformation journey can be long, complex and expensive. It can also be risky as recent studies show 85% of early DT projects have not delivered their promised results and 50% failed outright.

There are no guaranteed guidebooks or perfect paths for this journey. No wonder the early pioneers are saying the further we go, the less we know.

So it's vital that Change Leaders use an approach that can carry their whole organisation, Staff, Customers, Suppliers as well as other Stakeholders through a lengthy period of continuous transition, learning and adaptation.'

There is a lot to navigate through and the multiple demands on leaders will only increase. This raises the question as to whether we have the right leaders in place who can handle these turbulent and opportunity rich times, or are we in the process of developing them?

Leadership is viewed by many academics as being a contested set of ideas and theories. The great upside of this, of course, is that there are several hundred thousand books on the subject each giving interesting windows into a multifaceted concept. What we do know and what is easily recognisable is that there exists both effective and ineffective leadership.

One of the dilemmas for organisations in this ever-changing seascape is who they let onto the bridge (into the boardroom). The appointment of leaders, which often reflects what the organisation thinks it needs, has been interesting over the past couple of years. There have emerged some patterns, which almost reflect two extreme views.

1 There has been a temptation amongst the uncertainty to appoint or elect leaders who are certain about everything – or at least that is what they would have us believe. Their confidence to be able to fix everything says to some 'this is the strong person we have dreamt about and answer to all of our hopes'. The attraction is obvious and does allow people to create either heroes or villains. I do however lament our ability to suspend everything we know on occasion to go with leaders who have an almost sociopathic approach to leadership and change.

2 On the other hand I have also observed that some organisations who do understand these changing times appoint leaders who spend their time talking about how complex everything is and yet seem to do nothing much to take everyone forward.

Both extremes are dangerous and pose significant risks. The middle ground is occupied by women and men who want to do a good job and are probably wondering what this new landscape/seascape means for them. In order to understand fully what is going on in their system they collaborate with many and shift conversations from discussions to dialogue. They then are better placed to take good and timely decisions. How this then interfaces with AI processes that are also making decisions needs to be figured out fairly soon.

So perhaps we need to rethink what leadership means in these incredible times we are living through.

Having spent a lifetime developing leadership in many different contexts, I believe that at the very least we will need to add some additional skill areas to the capability mix, as well as developing some really important characteristics. Most importantly, I suspect too that the notion of what makes effective leadership will also need to go through some form of transformation of understanding.

I welcome therefore Fred Kiel's book based on extensive research called Return on Character (2015). He provides the evidence and link between a leader's character and financial organisational performance.

I was asked recently what specifically I saw as the emerging territory of leadership that we need to respond to. This is still a live area for discussions arising from conversations with colleagues and friends but already there are some identifiable touch points coming into focus and these include the following:

- Learning to navigate in uncharted waters is totally reliant on being first highly competent in navigational principles. This needs training, development, coaching, mentoring and assessment around the three core navigational foundations and related areas.

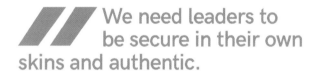

We need leaders to be secure in their own skins and authentic.

- There is a case to be made for senior leaders who are particularly responsible for delivering change programmes to be qualified and have up to date certification in change leadership.

- A shift is required towards being behaviourally and attitudinally collaborative as well as being structurally collaborative. This is key to understanding depth and range which informs decision making and taking.

- Leadership is fundamentally relational.

- Disruptive technology needs to have 'disruptive behaviour' with it in order to unfreeze some systemic patterns, allowing the new ways and ideas to become embedded. What often limits the full impact of technological advantage is where the behaviour of people remains as it always has been. The British navy of old only became effective when they adopted some of the buccaneer principles which emphasised purpose and stakeholding in the prize being sought.

- Reforming or at least re-examining political processes that block real collaboration by sustaining the adversarial treasury relationship that is echoed in the finance functions of local government. This is a big ask but unless these are reformed the required collaborative effort will be made null and void by departmental mentality.

- We need leaders to be secure in their own skins and authentic.

- A way needs to be found of sifting out sociopathic and psychopathic leaders at selection stage. (Their stock in trade is offering false and dangerous illusion of certainty wrapped up in charming tones.)

- Resilience has to become more prominent in all we do in the realm of change.

- Leaders should be able to apply the 'Compass of four Intelligences' based on John Dickson's superb work (personal communication).

- Decision making and taking should interface positively with AI and autonomous systems. This will include examining range, speed, content, process, checks, overrides and escalation routes.

- AI decisions need to be set alongside the political reality. This must include a discussion that is informed by our system of democracy.

- Leadership requires a deep understanding of change-related fields such as neuroscience, systems thinking, cultural fractals, history and so on, particularly the 'intertidal' and transitionary zones.

- There should be a greater emphasis on leaders being able to read in both the 'here and now and the 'there and then'. This will take in scenario thinking and application and takes this to new levels of skill.

- Leading geographically dispersed/digitally enabled teams should be part of the skill set, together with its implications for performance management.

- There will likely be a blurring of the leader/follower boundaries (i.e. increased emphasis on high-performing teams and self-reliant employees and team leaders). This paradoxically increases the need for greater clarity around other important boundaries including empowerment – particularly authority and accountability.

- There must be a relentless goal to hold leaders to account, like those responsible for navigation at sea.

- There needs to be a shift away from CV-motivated and time-limited appointments. Leaders should be committed as far as is possible for the duration of the change. Currently some highly influential roles only exist for between 3 and 9 months.

- There is a need to help buyers in the public sector become more informed and savvy when purchasing digital solutions.

- There is a greater need for leaders to understand 'end to end' life processes and programmes within their organisations.

- A new relationship with the 'third sector' is emerging and this is a potentially positive and a different form of stakeholding in local affairs. An example of this has been achieved in Southampton which brought together charities, businesses, faith groups, council members and officers and service users to create new approaches to tackling homelessness.

- In the public sector the issue is who really holds the vision? Is it central government, local government, individual service areas? There is a significant indication that leaders don't understand Navigational Principle 2 or are unwilling to apply it.

- Greater collaboration and sharing of technology will inevitably lead to legal issues about who owns the intellectual property rights. This has already hampered work between some of the UK's leading engineering companies.

- There must be an intelligent public debate about the ethics of technology and its use. Society must be able to play its part in creating boundaries and protocols.

The above is just a 'first take' on some of the areas that the development, assessment and appointment of leaders will have to take account of over the next few years. I have a feeling that the authors and gurus of leadership practice are going to be busy.

And here lies a challenge. Technological advances are being made at enormous speed and it is likely that when and if autonomous AI kicks in, this speed will increase still further. We therefore need to equip our leaders at a similar pace (or as near to it as we can humanly get) to be able to navigate with the capability required. The US navy has discovered what happens when the speed of technological advance leaves behind the capability of human systems. We all need to learn lessons from this and take fast corrective action in order that the technological dream doesn't become the nightmare that Stephen Hawking (2016) has flagged up.

Throughout the sections in this book I hope I have given some encouragement that it is indeed possible to navigate well in these challenging and opportunity-rich times. It all stems from a mastery of the three core navigational principles applied in the emerging reality of today's workforce.

Going into the next decades I hope we will find or develop men and women who are good at finding their way and taking others with them because as the WEF (2016) comments on their founder's vision: 'In particular Schwab (2015) calls for leaders and citizens to "together shape a future, that works for all by putting people first empowering them and constantly reminding ourselves that all new technologies are first and foremost tools made by people for people".'

Completeness in diversity

What leaders add magically into the mix is themselves, with all of their strengths and foibles. There is no such thing as the fully complete leader, just those on the journey who are described by Bennis (1989) as being 'real and authentic' or by Collins (2001, 2006) as being 'great'.

I am pleased also that none of us are complete as it means that we have to rely on others for the skills and abilities we lack, as well being able to offer the attributes we have.

I introduced Robert Arthur Hale at the beginning of this work as one of the influential figures in my story. Along with his pursuit of excellence and desire to give people a break in life, he could be cantankerous and driven. But I hold him in high regard nonetheless. Often, our weaknesses are simply strengths overplayed. I have never met a perfect leader but I have had the privilege of working with some exceptional women and men who are the real deal.

Every leader who is authentic will overlay everything that has been explored in this book with their style, gifts and weaknesses. Figuring out how to be the best they can be in their unique fashion and approach and then learning to flex enough to engage with others with different drivers will be very important.

There is still something I like about Jim Collins' research that asserts that demonstrably effective leadership has at its core two characteristics: fierce determination combined with humility.

Smart leaders play to their strengths and have close colleagues and friends to cover for their weaknesses. This requires real wisdom, courage and of course... trust.

No leader will be perfect but greatness and perfection are two different things. However all effective leaders and their teams will have to be skilled navigators and use, with maturity, the three principles I have explored in this book.

It all comes back to the three principles of navigation

For those who are either going through, or about to start on a change programme, it is reasonable expectation of the leadership that they are able to figure out (a) where they are; (b) where they want to get to; and (c) how to create an intelligent and dynamic programme to make it so.

These fundamentals will need to take a greater prominence in the range of development work over the next couple of decades. I would also like to see those of us in business and organisational life hold our leaders to account around these three principles much more rigorously than at present. At sea this keeps all minds focused.

I hope I have also illustrated that there is more to navigation than perhaps is apparent at first hand. This breadth and depth needs translating into our rapidly changing world. Hopefully too this book and some of the questions posed will have stimulated alternative perspectives and insights that will go on to start some interesting conversations.

I would recommend that if this work is used by a leadership team, the reviews and exploration are best done section by section so that important lessons aren't missed in the overall sweep of the area. If you would like any further information about this work or other papers mentioned do contact me on my email: chrislever@teleiosconsulting.com

> What leaders add magically into the mix is themselves, with all of their strengths and foibles. There is no such thing as the fully complete leader.

Section notes

1 Explanation of statistics quoted. One of the principles critical to all navigators to both understand and take account of, is the subject of error. This I have covered in the text in some detail. In essence this recognises that in attempts to define accurately a position, error will have potentially crept in from a number of places. This is why we as seafarers always triangulate information, using multiple sources of data to manage this.

In a similar way, in quoting success and failure rates of change programmes I have used multiple published studies that in the main seem to suggest a similar range. Of course there is some variance between the research and that is to be expected. The studies quoted in this book, and referenced, come from credible academic institutions.

The question is, how accurate is this data? This is a good and important question. I am aware that at the current time, some are beginning to challenge the reliability of these often quoted figures. I welcome this, as we do need to be rigorous. There are very obvious areas in change programmes where error can indeed creep in. This includes how we define success criteria over an extended time line, sampling procedures and processes, interpretation of the information and personal bias, just to name a few. This is why it is right to challenge the data.

So with this in mind and to be accountable for the figures I use in this book, I have used 3 primary sources to triangulate success and failure rates of change initiatives. Firstly I have used the figures from a very wide range of studies that suggests broad agreement between unrelated studies. I know too that these may all contain common errors of analysis and interpretation so my second positional fix is to use the data from the Change Ability study described over. This longitudinal and quantitative research is an important source of information. Its uniqueness lies in its ability to measure with some precision. My third point of triangulation is personal experience. I have worked in many sectors and in many places for a lot of years. Some of this work has afforded me the opportunity to simply observe how change is conducted. On a few occasions I have been involved in stabilising a programme of change that has been initiated to retain control of rapid and, almost, out of control growth. Often times I have been brought in because something has been missed in the planning stages. Most commonly I have been used to try and get back in to some kind of order a programme that has gone very 'wobbly' or is just plain failing. Across all of these experiences of the past few decades, have emerged common themes and a common range of success and failure rates.

So putting these three sources of information together is where I get the figures I quote. As a navigational principle I need to be as accurate as the specific situation requires me to be. So with the debate about the legitimacy of some of the published studies gathering apace there is a danger that we all end up driving for a final agreed percentage point that we can all quote and miss the very real fact that we all need to be much better at handling change and transformation. This is what this book is fundamentally about.

2 Change Ability refers to a unique longitudinal internet based study, started in 2000, that collects measurable data to answer the following question:

'In these turbulent times, how does an organisation change itself time and time again? And how does it do this faster and more successfully than its competitors?'

This research, which is still collecting information today, has identified four organisational change types – Change-Able, Change-Ineffective, Change-Dependent and Change-Inept. Only the 10-20% (a figure that shows a range over time) are able to fully deliver on the intended performance increases; the rest fail to fully meet expectations. Change-Inept organisations fail spectacularly. Currently this represents 50% of all Digital Transformation programmes in the public sector. The robustness of the study lies in its ability to measure specific elements around: Leadership; Selection of the right targets; Creating an appropriate structure; Developing an inhouse change capability; and Creating an effective change culture. The last of these was by far the most influential in regard to future success.

The study allows an organisation to benchmark performance, to diagnose the current state and form a customised programme of development to fix what needs fixing and maintain, that which is working well. This is all based on measurable and quantifiable data, which is what makes this research quite unique. Obviously the high commercial value of such data means that access to it is limited at this time but you can access it on request. To do so contact Steve Grudgings, a director of ChangeAbility Ltd, on his personal email address: steve.grudgings @btinternet.com

3 Compass of 4 Intelligences. I came across this concept authored by John Dickson back in 2006 when we were delivering an open programme for senior managers at Cranfield University. A team of us had been asked by the Business School to anticipate what it might be like working in digitalised and rapidly transforming businesses. We were interested in the challenges that would be created around flexible working, increased access to data, communication, politics, power and influence. On the back of this we designed and delivered a programme which explored and trained leaders in some of the new ways that needed to operate. We were very aware at the time we were working in a fast changing and emergent world with incredible opportunities and challenges. One theme that was consistent from leaders going through the programme was an increasing feeling of being disorientated and sensing that power had shifted in both its nature and location. The old ways were no longer working as well. Digitalisation had democratised access to information and flexible working was altering working practice and even the exercise of top down power in traditional hierarchical organisations was being challenged. A

common feeling expressed by leaders was that they had become everything to everybody and had lost a sense of themselves. They told us that they had lost their sharpness and their lightness of spirit. It was against this background that John Dickson began to play with the notion of the compass. Emotional Intelligence had begun to make a huge difference to people and relationships and yet there were some gaps too. It was clear that to succeed in this new and emerging world people had to actively keep up to date with rapid advancements in their business area. It was clear too that politics had not gone away although the nature of the game had shifted. Leaders told us that their dilemma was how to figure out what politically was going on and yet not get sucked into becoming just another player. Probably the most important aspect that leaders were describing to us was a loss of their own inner sense of what was important in a bigger scheme of life. Hence John came up with the notion of the compass of 4 intelligences based on the cardinal points of SQ, PQ, BQ and EQ. This idea, although never published, had great resonance with leaders and made a real difference too. I feel it is of significant worth at this time which is why it is included in this book. If you would like more information on this contact John Dickson through his website at www.dancehammer.co.uk and he will provide some background as well describe some of the pioneering work he is currently involved with.

References

Atticus (n.d.). ChangeAbility research, ongoing. Information available from Steve Grudgings on steve.grudgings@btinternet.com

Atticus Research (n.d.) Changeability longitudinal study (ongoing). For more information contact Ross Harling at Ross@rossharling.com

Babiak, Paul, & Hare, Robert D. (2006). Snakes in Suits. Regan. ISBN 978-0060837723.

Bell, Derrick (2002). Ethical Ambition. Bloomsbury. ISBN 978-0747564546.

Bennis, Warren (1989). On Becoming a Leader. Random House. ISBN 978-0099269392.

Collins, Jim (2001). Good to Great. Random House. ISBN 978-0712676090.

Collins, Jim (2006). Good to Great and the Social Sectors. ISBN 978-1905211326.

Collins, Jim, & Porras, Jerry I. (1996). 'Building Your Company's Vision,' Harvard Business Review, Sept–Oct.

Daily Mail (2010). '"It's bloody marvellous": British aid worker kidnapped at gunpoint in Somalia is freed after six days.' Daily Mail online, 20 October, at http://www.dailymail.co.uk/news/article-1322088/British-aid-worker-Frans-Barnard-kidnapped-Somalia-freed-6-days.html

Harling, Ross (2017a). Will your Council be a Digital Dynamo or Dinosaur?. LinkedIn post, 6 December. Available from the author at Ross@rossharling.com

Harling, Ross (2017b). 'A Footnote for the Future', 11 October. Unpublished article available from the author at Ross@rossharling.com

Hawking, Stephen (2016). 'This Is the Most Dangerous Time for Our Planet', Guardian, 1 Dec. Available from https://www.theguardian.com/commentisfree/2016/dec/01/stephen-hawking-dangerous-time-planet-inequality

Iarocci, Joe (2015) 'Why Are There So Many Leadership Books?' Blog at https://serveleadnow.com/why-are-there-so-many-leadership-books/

Ilbury, Chantell, & Sunter, Clem (2001). Mind of a Fox: Scenario Planning in Action. Human & Rousseau. ISBN 978-0798141697.

Kiel, Fred (2017). 'Return on Character', Harvard Business Review Press. ISBN 13 978-1-62527-130-3.

Kubler-Ross, Elizabeth (1970). On Death and Dying: What the Dying Have to Teach Doctors, Nurses, Clergy and Their Own Families. Tavistock Publications. ISBN 978-203889657.

Lenconi, Patrick (2002). Five Dysfunctions of a Team. Jossey- Bass. ISBN 978-0787960759.

Lever, Chris (2017). Ensuring Change Delivers Success: An 'End to End' View of the Process. Teleios Consulting. Available from the author at chrislever@teleiosconsulting.com. A revised edition of this book will be available at the start of 2019 (ISBN 978-1-9996282-2-2).

Martin, Roger L. (2016). 'M&A: The One Thing You Need to Get Right', Executive Summary. Harvard Business Review, June.

Schwab, Klaus (2015). 'The Fourth Industrial Revolution: What It Means and How to Respond'. Foreign Affairs, 12 December. Available at http://www.vassp.org.au/webpages/Documents2016/PDevents/The%20Fourth%20Industrial%20Revolution%20by%20Klaus%20Schwab.pdf

Stashwick, Stephen (2017). 'US Navy Reports on Collisions in Pacific – the USS John S. McCain'. The Diplomat. Available from https://thediplomat.com/2017/11/us-navy-reports-on-collisions-in-pacific-the-uss-john-s-mccain/

Taylor, Tim (2006). The Time Team: What Happened When, Section 8 Viking/Late Anglo-Saxon. Channel 4 Books. ISBN 978-1905026098.

Villiers, Alan (1973). Set of the Sails. Macmillan, first published 1950. ISBN 978-0330029902.

World Economic Forum (2016). 'The Fourth Industrial Revolution by Klaus Schwab'. Review available at https://www.weforum.org/about/the-fourth-industrial-revolution-by-klaus-schwab.